PRAISE FOR LUKE MARSH

From *"100+ Unexplained Mysteries for Curious Minds:"*

Luke Marsh's "100+ Unexplained Mysteries for Curious Minds" is an enthralling and informative journey through the most captivating enigmas of our world. It is a must-read for anyone with a thirst for knowledge and a fascination with the unexplained. Whether you're a skeptic seeking to challenge your beliefs or a believer seeking validation, this book offers an irresistible invitation to explore the uncharted territories of the mind. Delve into its pages, and prepare to be mystified.

— ROGER MARTINEZ

If you have a curious mind like me, "100+ Unexplained Mysteries for Curious Minds" is a must-read. From UFOs to lost civilizations, this book has a bit of everything. The author, Luke Marsh, definitely did his homework. The narratives are intriguing and detailed. A fascinating read that keeps you turning the pages. Solid 5 stars!

— CHRISTOFER

I'd like to use this book to plan future vacations to visit many of the places the author talks about! Each section is well written and researched, and I really enjoyed the author's commentary on the psychological and social aspects of the different events throughout the book.

— AMANDA

100+ MYTHICAL CREATURES FOR CURIOUS PEOPLE

100+ MYTHICAL CREATURES FOR CURIOUS PEOPLE

A JOURNEY THROUGH TIME AND CULTURES EXPLORING OVER 100 LEGENDARY BEASTS, MYSTICAL MONSTERS, MALEVOLENT ENTITIES, AND MORE

THE ULTIMATE 100 SERIES

LUKE MARSH

Book
Bound Studios

To all those who dare to dream, to believe in the impossible, and to journey into the realms of the fantastical. This book is dedicated to you, the explorers of the mythical and the magical, the seekers of the unknown, and the lovers of stories that transcend time and space. May you find in these pages a world that sparks your imagination, stirs your curiosity, and inspires you to keep the magic alive.

Fantasy is a necessary ingredient in living, it's a way of looking at life through the wrong end of a telescope, and that enables you to laugh at life's realities.

— DR. SEUSS

CONTENTS

From the Author xvii
Introduction to the World of Mythical Creatures xix

1. LEGENDARY BEASTS OF ANCIENT MYTHOLOGY 1
The Mighty Griffin: Guardian of Treasures 3
The Fearsome Chimera: A Monstrous Hybrid 4
The Enigmatic Sphinx: Riddles and Wisdom 5
The Ferocious Nemean Lion: A Herculean Challenge 7
The Cunning Lernaean Hydra: A Serpent with Many Heads 8
The Majestic Pegasus: The Winged Horse of the Gods 9
The Formidable Minotaur: A Labyrinth's Deadly Secret 11
The Fabled Phoenix: A Symbol of Rebirth and Immortality 12
The Elusive Unicorn: A Creature of Purity and Grace 13
The Terrifying Kraken: A Sea Monster of Epic Proportions 15
The Enduring Legacy of Ancient Mythological Beasts 16

2. ENIGMATIC CREATURES OF EUROPEAN FOLKLORE 19
The Enchanting Selkies: Shape-Shifting Seal People 21
The Elusive Kelpie: The Shape-Shifting Water Horse 22
The Mischievous Leprechaun: Ireland's Legendary Trickster 23
The Mysterious Will-o'-the-Wisp: The Deceptive Lights of the Marsh 25
The Terrifying Gorgon: The Deadly Stare of Medusa 26
The Cunning Basilisk: The King of Serpents 27
The Alluring Siren: The Deadly Song of the Sea 28
The Enigmatic Black Dog: The Omen of Death 30
The Enduring Legacy of European Mythical Creatures 31

3. MYSTICAL MONSTERS OF ASIAN LEGENDS 33
The Nine-Tailed Fox: Cunning and Enchantment 35
The Nian: A Beast of New Year's Lore 36
The Qilin: A Symbol of Prosperity and Virtue 37

The Jiangshi: The Hopping Undead 38
The Garuda: The Majestic Bird-God 40
The Rakshasa: Demons of Ancient India 41
The Kappa: The Mischievous River Imp 43
The Aswang: Shape-Shifting Predators of the Philippines 44
The Naga: Serpents of Wisdom and Power 45
The Tengu: The Mysterious Mountain Spirits 47
The Enduring Legacy of Asian Mythical Creatures 48

4. FEARSOME BEINGS OF AFRICAN MYTHOLOGY 51
The Grootslang: The Giant Serpent-Elephant Hybrid 53
The Tokoloshe: The Mischievous and Malicious Dwarf 54
The Adze: The Shape-Shifting Vampire 55
The Ninki Nanka: The Dragon-Like Swamp Dweller 57
The Bouda: The Werehyena Shapeshifter 58
The Impundulu: The Lightning Bird of Doom 59
The Mami Wata: The Enchanting Water Spirit 61
The Popobawa: The Terrifying Bat-Like Creature 62
The Yumboes: The Silver-Haired Spirits of the Forest 63
The Kongamato: The Prehistoric Flying Terror 65
The Enduring Legacy of Africa's Fearsome Beings 66

5. FANTASTICAL CREATURES OF THE AMERICAS 69
The Thunderbird: A Powerful Symbol of Native American Lore 71
The Wendigo: The Terrifying Cannibalistic Spirit of the North 72
The Chupacabra: The Mysterious Bloodsucking Creature of Latin America 74
The Skinwalker: The Shape-Shifting Sorcerers of Navajo Legend 75
The Pukwudgie: The Mischievous Little People of Wampanoag Folklore 77
The Quetzalcoatl: The Feathered Serpent Deity of Mesoamerican Mythology 78
The Sasquatch: The Enigmatic Giant Hominid of North American Forests 79
The La Llorona: The Weeping Woman of Mexican Folklore 81
The Cadejo: The Dueling Canine Spirits of Central American Legends 82

The Jersey Devil: The Fearsome Beast of the Pine Barrens 83
The Enduring Legacy of the Americas' Mythical Creatures 84

6. OCEANIC AND AQUATIC MYTHICAL CREATURES 87
Mermaids and Mermen: The Alluring Half-Human, Half-Fish Beings 89
The Loch Ness Monster: Scotland's Mysterious Water Dweller 90
The Leviathan: The Ancient Sea Serpent of Biblical Lore 92
Jormungandr: The World Serpent of Norse Mythology 93
Charybdis and Scylla: The Deadly Duo of Greek Mythology 94
The Aspidochelone: The Gigantic Sea Turtle of Medieval Legends 96
The Bunyip: The Fearsome Creature of Australian Aboriginal Mythology 97
The Enduring Fascination with Oceanic and Aquatic Mythical Creatures 98

7. HYBRID CREATURES: COMBINATIONS OF THE FAMILIAR AND THE STRANGE 101
The Centaur: Half-Human, Half-Horse Warriors 103
The Manticore: A Deadly Mix of Lion, Human, and Scorpion 104
The Harpy: Fierce and Terrifying Bird-Women 105
The Satyr: Mischievous and Lustful Half-Human, Half-Goat Beings 106
The Enduring Fascination with Hybrid Creatures in Mythology 108

8. DIVINE AND CELESTIAL BEINGS: MYTHICAL CREATURES OF THE HEAVENS 111
The Mighty Gods and Goddesses: Rulers of the Heavens 113
Angels and Archangels: Messengers and Protectors of the Divine 114
The Celestial Dragons: Guardians of the Cosmic Balance 116
The Valkyries: Choosers of the Slain and Guides to the Afterlife 117
The Cherubim and Seraphim: The Highest Orders of Angelic Beings 119

The Celestial Beasts: Mythical Creatures of the Chinese Constellations 120
The Apsaras and Gandharvas: Celestial Dancers and Musicians of Hindu Mythology 122
The Enduring Legacy of Divine and Celestial Beings in Mythology 123

9. DARK AND MALEVOLENT ENTITIES: CREATURES OF THE UNDERWORLD 125
The Demonic Hierarchy: Rulers of the Underworld 127
Vampires: The Undead Predators of the Night 128
Werewolves: Shape-shifting Beasts of Legend 130
Ghouls and Revenants: The Restless Dead 131
The Nuckelavee: A Horrifying Hybrid of Man and Beast 133
The Dybbuk: Possessing Spirits of the Damned 134
The Strigoi: The Soul-Stealing Wraiths of Eastern Europe 135
The Enduring Allure of Dark Mythical Creatures 136

10. THE ROLE OF MYTHICAL CREATURES IN MODERN CULTURE AND MEDIA 139
Mythical Creatures in Literature: From Ancient Epics to Modern Bestsellers 141
The Silver Screen: How Cinema Brought Mythical Creatures to Life 142
Television and the Rise of Fantasy Series: A New Platform for Mythical Beings 144
The World of Gaming: Interactive Encounters with Mythical Creatures 145
Art and Design: The Aesthetic Influence of Mythical Beings 147
Fashion and Mythology: The Inspiration Behind Trendsetting Styles 149
The Role of Mythical Creatures in Advertising and Branding 150
Mythical Creatures as Cultural Symbols: National Identity and Heritage 152
The Psychological Impact of Mythical Creatures on Society 153
The Future of Mythical Creatures in Media: New Technologies and Storytelling Techniques 155
The Timeless Significance of Mythical Creatures in Modern Culture and Media 156

The Enduring Fascination with Mythical Creatures 159

About the Author 167
From the Author 169

INTRODUCTION TO THE WORLD OF MYTHICAL CREATURES

Welcome to a realm where the boundaries of reality and imagination blur, the ordinary meets the extraordinary, and the known world gives way to the mysterious and the magical. This is the enchanting world of mythical creatures, a realm that has captivated the human spirit since the dawn of time. These fantastical beings have been woven into the fabric of our collective consciousness, shaping our beliefs, stories, and dreams. They have been the protagonists of countless legends, the muses of great artists, and the inspiration for numerous works of literature, music, and film.

As you embark on this journey through the pages of this book, you will encounter creatures of all shapes and sizes, from the majestic and awe-inspiring to the sinister and terrifying. You will meet beings that have been revered as gods and those that have been feared as demons. You will explore the rich tapestry of myths and legends that have given birth to these creatures, delving into the depths of human imagination and the boundless creativity that has brought them to life.

In this world of mythical creatures, you will find not only the familiar figures of Greek, Roman, and Norse mythology but also the lesser-known beings that have emerged from the folklore of cultures across the globe. From the ancient civilizations of Mesopotamia and

Egypt to the indigenous tribes of the Americas, Africa, and Oceania, you will discover a diverse array of mythical beings that reflect the unique beliefs, values, and fears of the people who created them.

As you immerse yourself in this captivating realm, you will appreciate the power of myth and the enduring appeal of these fantastical creatures. They are not merely the products of human imagination but also the embodiment of our deepest desires, greatest fears, and most profound questions about the nature of existence. They are the mirrors that reflect our humanity, the windows that offer a glimpse into the mysteries of the universe, and the keys that unlock the secrets of our hearts.

So prepare to embark on a journey as we unveil the enchanting world of mythical creatures and invite you to explore the wonders that lie within. Let your imagination soar, your curiosity be piqued, and your sense of wonder be awakened as you delve into the pages of this book and discover the magic that awaits you.

A Glimpse into the Origins of Myth and Legend

Since the dawn of human civilization, myths and legends have been integral to our collective consciousness. These captivating stories passed down through generations, have served as a means to understand the world around us and our place within it. They have shaped our beliefs, values, and traditions and have provided a foundation for our cultural identity.

The origins of myth and legend can be traced back to the earliest human societies, where oral storytelling was the primary means of preserving history and knowledge. The natural world often inspired these tales, as our ancestors sought to explain the mysteries of life, death, and the cosmos. Over time, these stories evolved and became more complex, incorporating elements of religion, morality, and the supernatural.

Mythical creatures have always been at the heart of these stories, embodying the fears, desires, and aspirations of those who created them. From the mighty dragons of ancient China to the elusive unicorns of medieval Europe, these fantastical beings have captured our imagination and continue to enchant us today.

In many cases, mythical creatures served as symbols of the forces of nature, representing the power and unpredictability of the elements. For example, the thunderbird of Native American mythology was believed to control the weather, while the Greek god Poseidon was often depicted riding a sea monster to demonstrate his dominion over the oceans.

In other instances, mythical creatures were used to explore the complexities of human nature, reflecting our inner struggles and desires. For example, the werewolf, a creature that transforms from man to beast under the light of the full moon, can be seen as a metaphor for the duality of human existence, highlighting the constant battle between our rational and primal instincts.

As we delve into the world of mythical creatures, it is important to remember that these beings are not merely the product of human imagination but rather a reflection of our deepest fears, hopes, and dreams. They provide a window into the human psyche, revealing the timeless themes and universal truths that connect us all.

In this book, we will embark on a fascinating journey through the rich tapestry of mythical beings from various cultures and time periods. We will explore their origins, significance, and enduring appeal that continues to captivate the hearts and minds of people worldwide. So, let us begin our adventure into the enchanting world of mythical creatures and discover the magic within these timeless tales.

Exploring the Rich Tapestry of Mythical Beings

The primary purpose of this book is to take you on an enthralling journey through the captivating world of mythical creatures. These fantastical beings have captured the imaginations of countless generations, transcending time and culture to become an integral part of our collective consciousness. By delving into the rich tapestry of myth and legend, we aim not only to entertain and inform but also to foster a deeper appreciation for the power of storytelling and the human imagination.

Throughout history, mythical creatures have been symbols of our deepest fears, desires, and aspirations. They have been used to explain the unexplainable, teach moral lessons, and inspire awe and wonder. By exploring the stories and lore surrounding these mysterious beings, we can gain valuable insights into the human experience and the universal themes that connect us all.

This book is designed to be both a comprehensive guide and an engaging narrative, weaving together the fascinating tales of mythical creatures worldwide. From the majestic dragons of the East to the elusive mermaids of the deep, we will uncover the secrets and mysteries surrounding these incredible beings. Along the way, we will encounter the heroes and villains, gods and monsters, who have shaped our understanding of these mythical creatures and their enduring allure.

So, prepare yourself for an unforgettable adventure as we journey through the enchanting world of mythical creatures. Together, we will discover the magic, mystery, and wonder at the heart of our most cherished legends and the enduring appeal of the fantastical beings that inhabit them.

Embracing the Endless Allure of the Fantastical

As we reach the end of this introductory chapter, we must recognize the timeless charm and allure of mythical creatures. These fantastical beings have captured the imaginations of countless generations, transcending cultural and geographical boundaries. They have been immortalized in stories, art, and even religious beliefs, as powerful symbols of our collective human experience.

The world of mythical creatures is vast and diverse, offering a rich tapestry of legends and lore that can both entertain and educate. By delving into the stories of these mysterious beings, we gain a deeper understanding of the cultures that created them and the universal themes that connect us all. Fear, love, heroism, and the eternal struggle between good and evil are threads that weave together the intricate tapestry of myth and legend.

My lifelong passion for mythology has led me on countless adventures through the realms of the fantastical. I have been continually amazed by the depth and complexity of the stories I have encountered and the enduring appeal of the creatures that inhabit them. This book will serve as a gateway for readers to embark on their journeys of discovery, unearthing the hidden treasures in the world of mythical creatures.

In the following chapters, we will embark on a comprehensive journey through cultures and time, exploring the origins, characteristics, and stories of one hundred mythical creatures. From the majestic dragons of the East to the enigmatic sphinxes of ancient Egypt, each creature will be brought to life through vivid descriptions and captivating tales. Along the way, we will also delve into the historical and cultural contexts that have shaped these myths, shedding light on the enduring power of the human imagination.

As you navigate the pages of this book, I invite you to embrace the endless allure of the fantastical. Allow yourself to be transported to distant lands and ancient times, where heroes and gods walk among the creatures of myth and legend. Open your mind to the wonders of the unknown, and let the enchanting world of mythical creatures awaken your sense of curiosity and wonder.

So prepare yourself for an unforgettable adventure as we enter the captivating realm of mythical creatures. May the stories and legends that await you inspire your imagination and ignite your passion for the fantastical.

1

LEGENDARY BEASTS OF ANCIENT MYTHOLOGY

An image of a majestic griffin guarding a treasure hoard.

Since the dawn of human civilization, mythical creatures have captivated our collective imagination, transcending the boundaries of time, culture, and geography. These legendary beasts, born from the depths of our ancestral fears and desires, have been woven into the very fabric of our myths, legends, and folklore. They symbolize our hopes, dreams, and deepest fears, embodying the eternal struggle between good and evil, chaos and order, and life and death.

The allure of mythical beasts lies in their ability to transport us to a world beyond our mundane reality, where the impossible becomes possible, and the ordinary becomes extraordinary. These creatures challenge our understanding of the natural world, defying the laws of physics and biology, and inviting us to explore the limits of our imagination. They represent the untamed forces of nature, the mysteries of the cosmos, and the hidden depths of the human psyche.

In this chapter, we will embark on a thrilling journey through the annals of ancient mythology, unearthing the stories and legends that have shaped our understanding of these enigmatic beings. From the mighty Griffin, guardian of treasures, to the fearsome Chimera, a monstrous hybrid of lion, goat, and serpent, we will delve into the rich tapestry of myth and symbolism that surrounds these fascinating creatures.

We will encounter the enigmatic Sphinx, whose riddles and wisdom have confounded travelers for millennia, and the ferocious Nemean Lion, whose defeat was one of the legendary Hercules' greatest challenges. We will witness the cunning of the Lernaean Hydra, a serpent with many heads, and the majesty of Pegasus, the winged horse of the gods.

Our journey will take us through the labyrinthine corridors of the formidable Minotaur's lair and into the heart of the fabled Phoenix's fiery rebirth. We will discover the elusive Unicorn, a creature of purity and grace, and confront the terrifying Kraken, a sea monster of epic proportions.

As we explore the enduring legacy of these ancient mythological beasts, we will uncover the timeless truths and universal themes that continue to resonate with us today. For in the tales of these legendary creatures, we find a mirror that reflects our humanity, a window into the depths of our imagination, and a key to unlocking the secrets of our shared cultural heritage. So, let us embark on this wondrous adventure and step into the realm of the mythical beasts that have captivated our hearts and minds for generations.

The Mighty Griffin: Guardian of Treasures

In the vast and fascinating realm of mythical creatures, the mighty Griffin holds a special place as a symbol of power, wisdom, and protection. This majestic beast, with the body of a lion and the head and wings of an eagle, has captivated the imagination of countless generations, transcending cultural and geographical boundaries. As a guardian of treasures and a symbol of divine authority, the Griffin has left an indelible mark on the tapestry of ancient mythology.

The origins of the Griffin can be traced back to the ancient civilizations of the Near East, where it was revered as a sacred creature by the Sumerians, Assyrians, and Persians. The Griffin's unique combination of the lion, the king of beasts, and the eagle, the ruler of the skies, made it a potent symbol of strength and nobility. Moreover, this awe-inspiring creature was believed to be able to soar to great heights and traverse vast distances, making it an ideal guardian of the most precious and elusive treasures.

In Greek mythology, the Griffin was associated with the gods Apollo and Zeus, often depicted riding on its back or using it as a loyal steed. The Griffin was also believed to be the protector of the divine nectar, ambrosia, and the sacred gold mined by the Arimaspi, a tribe of one-eyed giants. The Griffin's fierce and relentless battle against these formidable adversaries was a testament to its unwavering loyalty and courage.

The Griffin's role as a guardian of treasures extended beyond mythology and into art and architecture. Throughout history, the image of the Griffin has adorned countless monuments, sculptures, and decorative objects, serving as a powerful symbol of protection and a deterrent against evil forces. In medieval Europe, the Griffin became a popular motif in heraldry, representing courage, vigilance, and strength.

The enduring appeal of the Griffin lies in its unique blend of majesty, mystery, and might. As a creature that embodies the best qualities of the lion and the eagle, the Griffin serves as a potent reminder of the power and wisdom that can be found in the natural world. Its role as a guardian of treasures, both material and spiritual, speaks to the human desire for protection and guidance in the face of life's challenges.

In conclusion, the mighty Griffin stands tall as one of the most captivating and enduring mythical creatures of ancient mythology. Its legacy as a guardian of treasures and a symbol of divine authority continues to inspire awe and wonder, reminding us of the timeless allure of the mythical beasts that have shaped our collective imagination.

The Fearsome Chimera: A Monstrous Hybrid

In the annals of ancient mythology, few creatures have captured the imagination, quite like the fearsome Chimera. This monstrous hybrid beast has long been a symbol of terror and chaos, embodying the darkest aspects of human fear and the unknown. With its unique amalgamation of different animals, the Chimera has become an enduring symbol of the power and mystery of the natural world.

The Chimera's origins can be traced back to the myths of ancient Greece, where it was said to be the offspring of the monstrous Typhon and Echidna, two fearsome creatures in their own right. The Chimera was described as having the body of a lion, the tail of a serpent, and the head of a goat, which was said to breathe fire. This bizarre combination of features made the Chimera a truly terrifying sight to behold, and it was believed to be an omen of disaster and misfortune.

In the ancient world, the Chimera was a symbol of the destructive power of nature, as well as the unpredictable and chaotic forces that governed the universe. Its fiery breath was said to be capable of laying waste to entire cities, and its fearsome appearance struck terror into the hearts of all who encountered it. The Chimera was also a symbol of the untamed wilderness, representing the dangers that lurked beyond the borders of civilization.

The Chimera's most famous appearance in mythology comes from the story of Bellerophon, a hero tasked with slaying the beast to test his courage and skill. With the help of the winged horse Pegasus, Bellerophon managed to defeat the Chimera by shooting it with a lead-tipped arrow, which melted in the creature's fiery breath and suffocated it. This tale of heroism and triumph over seemingly insurmountable odds has become a classic example of the human struggle against the forces of chaos and destruction.

Over the centuries, the Chimera has continued to be a popular subject in art and literature, with its fearsome visage and fiery breath serving as a potent symbol of the darker aspects of the human psyche. The Chimera has also become a metaphor for blending disparate elements, as its unique combination of animal features represents the merging of different realms of existence.

In conclusion, the fearsome Chimera is one of the most iconic and enduring mythical creatures in human history. Its monstrous hybrid form and destructive powers have made it a symbol of chaos, fear, and the untamed forces of nature. The Chimera's legacy continues to inspire awe and terror in equal measure, serving as a reminder of the power and mystery of the ancient world.

The Enigmatic Sphinx: Riddles and Wisdom

The Sphinx, an enigmatic creature of ancient mythology, has captivated the imagination of people for centuries. With a lion's body and a human's head, the Sphinx is a symbol of wisdom, mystery, and riddles. This legendary beast has its roots in both Egyptian and Greek mythology, and its tales have been passed down through generations, inspiring awe and wonder in those who hear them.

In Egyptian mythology, the Sphinx is known as a benevolent

guardian figure, often depicted as a male with the head of a pharaoh. These sphinxes were believed to protect sacred temples and tombs, warding off evil spirits and intruders. The most famous example of an Egyptian Sphinx is the Great Sphinx of Giza, a colossal limestone statue that stands guard over the Pyramids of Giza. This ancient monument, with its enigmatic gaze, has puzzled archaeologists and historians for centuries, as its true purpose and origin remain shrouded in mystery.

In contrast, the Greek Sphinx is portrayed as a cunning and malevolent creature, often depicted as a female with the wings of a bird. According to Greek mythology, the Sphinx was sent by the gods to plague the city of Thebes, where she perched on a high rock and posed a riddle to all who wished to enter the city. The riddle, which has become synonymous with the Sphinx, was as follows:

> *"Which creature has one voice and yet becomes four-footed and two-footed and three-footed?"*

The citizens of Thebes could not solve the riddle, and the Sphinx devoured all who failed to answer correctly. Finally, desperate for a solution, the people of Thebes turned to the hero Oedipus, who could decipher the enigmatic riddle. The answer was "man," who crawls on all fours as a baby, walks on two feet as an adult, and uses a cane as a third leg in old age. Upon hearing the correct answer, the Sphinx was so distraught that she threw herself from the rock, ending her reign of terror over Thebes.

The story of the Sphinx and her riddle has been immortalized in literature, art, and popular culture, serving as a testament to the power of wisdom and the human intellect. The enigmatic nature of the Sphinx continues to fascinate us as we seek to unravel the mysteries of this mythical creature and the ancient world from which it emerged.

In conclusion, the Sphinx is a legendary beast that embodies the allure of ancient mythology. Its tales of riddles and wisdom have captivated the human imagination for centuries, and its enigmatic presence inspires awe and wonder. As we delve deeper into the stories of the

Sphinx and other mythical creatures, we are reminded of the timeless appeal of these ancient legends and the enduring legacy they leave behind.

The Ferocious Nemean Lion: A Herculean Challenge

In the annals of ancient mythology, few creatures have captured the imagination, quite like the ferocious Nemean Lion. This legendary beast, known for its impenetrable hide and unparalleled strength, has become synonymous with an insurmountable challenge. As the first labor of the Greek hero Heracles (more commonly known as Hercules), the Nemean Lion is a testament to the enduring power of myth and the human spirit's ability to triumph over adversity.

The story of the Nemean Lion begins in the region of Nemea, a fertile valley in the Peloponnese of southern Greece. According to legend, this monstrous lion was the offspring of the primordial gods Typhon and Echidna, making it a sibling to other fearsome creatures such as the Chimera and the Lernaean Hydra. The Nemean Lion was said to terrorize the local inhabitants, devouring their livestock and leaving a trail of destruction in its wake.

When Heracles was tasked with completing twelve seemingly impossible labors as penance for his past transgressions, his first challenge was to slay the Nemean Lion. Recognizing the gravity of this undertaking, Heracles approached the task with cunning and brute force. He first attempted to shoot the lion with arrows, only to discover its golden fur impervious to such attacks. Undeterred, Heracles confronted the beast in its lair, a cave with two entrances.

Using his immense strength, Heracles blocked one of the cave's entrances with a large boulder, trapping the lion inside. He then entered the cave through the remaining entrance, armed with only a wooden club and his bare hands. In the cave's darkness, Heracles grappled with the Nemean Lion, eventually strangling the beast to death. As a testament to his victory, Heracles skinned the lion using its claws, sharp enough to pierce its impenetrable hide. He then donned the lion's pelt as a cloak, a symbol of his triumph and a reminder of the seemingly insurmountable challenge he had overcome.

The tale of the Nemean Lion and Heracles' victory over it is a powerful allegory for the human spirit's ability to conquer even the most daunting obstacles. The lion's fearsome reputation and seemingly invincible nature represent the challenges that we all face in our lives, while Heracles' determination and resourcefulness serve as a reminder that even the most formidable of foes can be vanquished through perseverance and ingenuity.

In conclusion, the story of the Nemean Lion and its defeat at the hands of Heracles is a timeless testament to the power of myth and the human spirit. As we continue to explore the pantheon of legendary beasts that populate the world of ancient mythology, the Nemean Lion stands as a shining example of the enduring allure of these fantastical creatures and the lessons they can teach us about our capacity for triumph in the face of adversity.

The Cunning Lernaean Hydra: A Serpent with Many Heads

The Lernaean Hydra, a fearsome and cunning serpent, has long captivated the imaginations of those who delved into ancient mythology. This monstrous creature, with its many heads and venomous breath, has become a symbol of resilience and adaptability and a formidable challenge for heroes to overcome.

Originating from Greek mythology, the Hydra was said to dwell in the swamps of Lerna, a region in the Peloponnese known for its connection to the underworld. The creature was born from the union of two primordial deities, Typhon and Echidna, responsible for spawning many of the most terrifying beasts in Greek myth. The Hydra was a truly nightmarish sight with its serpentine body and multiple heads.

The most famous encounter with the Lernaean Hydra comes from the tale of Heracles, also known as Hercules and his Twelve Labors. As the second of these labors, Heracles was tasked with slaying the Hydra, a seemingly impossible feat due to the creature's unique ability: whenever one of its heads was severed, two more would grow in its place. This made the Hydra an almost invincible opponent, as each attempt to vanquish it only made it stronger.

However, Heracles was not one to be easily deterred. With the help of his nephew, Iolaus, he devised a clever strategy to overcome the Hydra's regenerative powers. As Heracles cut off each head, Iolaus quickly cauterized the wound with a burning torch, preventing new heads from sprouting. The two defeated the seemingly invincible Hydra through their combined efforts, with Heracles dipping his arrows in the creature's venomous blood to make them even more deadly.

The tale of the Lernaean Hydra serves as a powerful allegory for the challenges we face in life. Like the Hydra, our problems can often seem insurmountable, growing and multiplying as we struggle to overcome them. However, with determination, ingenuity, and the help of others, we can conquer even the most daunting of obstacles.

In conclusion, the Lernaean Hydra is one of the most iconic and enduring mythical creatures in ancient mythology. Its cunning nature and unique abilities have made it a symbol of resilience and adaptability, while its defeat at the hands of Heracles serves as a testament to the power of human ingenuity and perseverance. As we continue to explore the world of mythical beasts, the Hydra remains a fascinating and inspiring example of the challenges and triumphs that define our shared human experience.

The Majestic Pegasus: The Winged Horse of the Gods

Few are as universally admired and cherished as the majestic Pegasus in the vast and wondrous pantheon of mythical creatures. This awe-inspiring winged horse has captured the imagination of countless generations, symbolizing freedom, power, and the boundless potential of the human spirit. As we delve into the ancient tales and legends surrounding this extraordinary beast, we will discover its profound impact on the art, literature, and culture of civilizations throughout history.

The origins of Pegasus can be traced back to the rich tapestry of Greek mythology. According to the ancient poets, Pegasus was born from the blood of the slain Gorgon Medusa, a monstrous creature with snakes for hair and a gaze that could turn men to stone. When the hero Perseus beheaded Medusa, Pegasus sprang forth from her severed neck, a miraculous birth that imbued the creature with an air of divine mystery.

From the moment of its creation, Pegasus was destined for greatness. With its mighty wings and unmatched speed, the horse quickly caught the gods' attention. The supreme deity Zeus, recognizing the unique abilities of Pegasus, chose the winged steed to be his mount and tasked it with carrying his thunderbolts. In this exalted role, Pegasus became a symbol of divine authority and the embodiment of the gods' dominion over the natural world.

Yet, the story of Pegasus is not limited to the realm of the gods. The creature also played a crucial part in the lives of several mortal heroes, most notably the legendary Bellerophon. With the aid of the goddess Athena, Bellerophon managed to tame Pegasus and ride the magnificent beast into battle against the fearsome Chimera. Together, they vanquished the monster and embarked on numerous other adventures, solidifying their place in the annals of mythological lore.

The enduring appeal of Pegasus lies in its unique combination of strength, beauty, and grace. As a creature transcending the earthbound world's limitations, Pegasus has come to represent the human desire to break free from the constraints of our mortal existence and soar to new heights of achievement and understanding. This timeless symbol of aspiration and transcendence continues to inspire artists, writers, and dreamers across the globe, reminding us of the limitless possibilities that await those who dare to spread their wings and take flight.

In conclusion, the majestic Pegasus is one of the most iconic and beloved mythical creatures ever. From its miraculous birth to its adventures with gods and heroes, this winged horse's story has captivated countless generations' hearts and minds. As we continue to explore ancient mythology's rich and diverse world, we can look to Pegasus as a shining example of the power of imagination and the enduring allure of the legendary beasts that populate our collective consciousness.

The Formidable Minotaur: A Labyrinth's Deadly Secret

In the annals of ancient mythology, few creatures have captured the imagination, quite like the formidable Minotaur. This monstrous hybrid, with the body of a man and the head of a bull, has long been a symbol of terror and the darker aspects of human nature. The Minotaur's tragic tale is one of hubris, punishment, and, ultimately, redemption.

The story of the Minotaur begins with King Minos of Crete, who prayed to the sea god Poseidon for a magnificent bull to solidify his claim to the throne. Poseidon granted his request but with one condition: the bull must be sacrificed in the god's honor. However, King Minos, blinded by greed and pride, chose to keep the majestic creature for himself, sacrificing a lesser bull in its place. Enraged by this betrayal, Poseidon cursed Minos' wife, Queen Pasiphae, to fall in love with the bull. This unnatural union resulted in the monstrous Minotaur, a creature that embodied the consequences of human arrogance and defiance of the gods.

Unable to control the beast's insatiable hunger for human flesh, King Minos commissioned the brilliant inventor Daedalus to construct an elaborate labyrinth to contain the Minotaur. With its twisting corridors and dead ends, this sprawling maze was designed to be virtually impossible to navigate, ensuring that the Minotaur would remain trapped within its walls. To appease the monster's appetite, Minos demanded that seven young men and seven young women be sent as tribute from Athens every nine years, a cruel reminder of the king's power and the price of disobedience.

The Minotaur's reign of terror would continue until the arrival of the Athenian hero Theseus, who volunteered to be part of the sacrificial tribute. With the help of Minos' daughter Ariadne, who had fallen in love with him, Theseus navigated the labyrinth using a ball of thread to mark his path. Finally, in a fierce battle, Theseus confronted the

Minotaur and conquered the beast with a mighty blow, ending its reign of terror and freeing the people of Athens from their terrible burden.

The story of the Minotaur serves as a cautionary tale, reminding us of the dangers of pride and the consequences of defying the natural order. Yet it also speaks to the power of human ingenuity and the potential for redemption, as Theseus' heroism ultimately transforms a symbol of terror into one of hope and liberation. The Minotaur's labyrinth, with its twisting passages and hidden secrets, remains an enduring metaphor for the complexities of the human psyche and the challenges we must overcome in our quest for self-discovery and personal growth.

The Fabled Phoenix: A Symbol of Rebirth and Immortality

The phoenix, a mythical bird of unparalleled beauty and splendor, has captivated the hearts and minds of people for centuries. This awe-inspiring creature is a symbol of rebirth and immortality and a testament to the resilience of the human spirit. In this section, we will delve into the enchanting world of the phoenix, exploring its origins, characteristics, and profound impact on various cultures throughout history.

The legend of the phoenix can be traced back to ancient Egypt, where it was known as the Bennu bird. This divine creature was believed to be the soul of the sun god Ra, and its appearance was said to herald a new era of prosperity and renewal. The Greeks later adopted the myth, giving the bird its now-famous name, "phoenix," which means "crimson" or "red-gold" in Greek. This name is a fitting tribute to the bird's vibrant plumage, which is said to shimmer with fiery red, orange, and gold hues.

The most striking aspect of the phoenix myth is its unique life cycle. According to legend, the phoenix lives for hundreds or even thousands of years before it reaches the end of its life. When this time comes, the bird builds a nest of fragrant spices and herbs, which it then sets ablaze. As the flames consume the nest and the phoenix within, a new, young phoenix rises from the ashes, reborn and ready to embark on its own long life. This remarkable process of death and rebirth has made the phoenix a powerful symbol of renewal, transformation, and the indomitable spirit of life.

Throughout history, the phoenix has been revered by various cultures and has found its way into numerous works of art, literature, and folklore. In ancient Rome, the phoenix was often depicted on coins and monuments, symbolizing the eternal nature of the empire. In Christianity, the phoenix has been used as a metaphor for the resurrection of Jesus Christ and the concept of spiritual rebirth. In Chinese mythology, the phoenix, or "fenghuang," symbolizes grace, virtue, and the union of yin and yang. It is often depicted alongside the dragon, representing the perfect balance of masculine and feminine energies.

The phoenix's ability to rise from the ashes has also made it a famous emblem of hope and resilience in the face of adversity. This majestic bird serves as a reminder that even in the darkest times, there is always the potential for new beginnings and the promise of a brighter future. Countless individuals and organizations have used its image to symbolize strength, perseverance, and the power of transformation.

In conclusion, the fabled phoenix is a remarkable mythical creature that has captured people's imagination across cultures and throughout the ages. Its unique life cycle and awe-inspiring beauty have made it a powerful symbol of rebirth, immortality, and the enduring spirit of life. As we continue exploring the fascinating world of mythical creatures, the phoenix stands as a shining example of the timeless allure and profound impact these legendary beasts have on our collective consciousness.

The Elusive Unicorn: A Creature of Purity and Grace

The unicorn, a creature of unparalleled beauty and purity, has captured the hearts and imaginations of countless generations. With its slender, graceful body and a single, spiraling horn adorning its forehead, the unicorn symbolizes innocence, magic, and enchantment. This mythical beast has its roots in ancient mythology, and its legend has been passed down through the ages, evolving and adapting to various cultures and beliefs.

The origins of the unicorn can be traced back to ancient civilizations such as the Indus Valley, Mesopotamia, and Greece. In these early cultures, the unicorn was often depicted as a powerful and majestic creature possessing magical and healing properties. Its horn, in particular, was believed to purify water, neutralize poison, and even cure diseases. As such, the unicorn was highly sought after, and its horn became a valuable and coveted commodity.

Throughout history, the unicorn has been portrayed in various forms, often as a symbol of purity and grace. In medieval Europe, it was believed that only a virgin maiden could tame a wild unicorn, and the creature would willingly lay its head in her lap. This image of the unicorn and the virgin became a famous allegory for the relationship between Christ and the Virgin Mary, further emphasizing the creature's association with purity and innocence.

In addition to its religious symbolism, the unicorn has been featured in numerous works of art, literature, and folklore. From the intricate tapestries of the Middle Ages to the fantastical tales of modern fantasy novels, the unicorn has remained a beloved and enduring figure in popular culture. Its elusive and mysterious nature has only served to heighten its allure, as countless tales recount the adventures of those who sought to capture or behold the magnificent creature.

Despite its mythical status, the unicorn has also been the subject of various scientific inquiries and debates. Throughout history, numerous explorers and naturalists have claimed to have discovered evidence of the creature's existence, often in the form of fossils or remains. While these claims have largely been debunked, they have contributed to the ongoing fascination with the unicorn and its place in the natural world.

In conclusion, the elusive unicorn remains a captivating and enduring figure in ancient mythology and beyond. Its graceful form and magical properties have inspired countless tales and works of art, while its symbolism of purity and innocence has resonated with people across cultures and generations. As a testament to the power of imagination and the allure of the unknown, the unicorn continues to enchant and inspire, leaving an indelible mark on the world of myth and legend.

The Terrifying Kraken: A Sea Monster of Epic Proportions

The vast and mysterious depths of the ocean have long been a source of fascination and fear for humankind. So it is no wonder that one of the most fearsome and awe-inspiring mythical creatures of ancient mythology is said to dwell beneath the waves: the terrifying Kraken. This colossal sea monster has captured the imaginations of sailors, writers, and artists for centuries, and its legend continues to endure in popular culture today.

The Kraken is believed to have originated in Norse mythology, where it was known as the "hafgufa" or "sea mist." According to ancient tales, this enormous beast was said to dwell off the coasts of Norway and Greenland, where it would wait for unsuspecting ships to pass by. Then, with its massive tentacles, the Kraken would drag the vessels and their hapless crews beneath the waves, never to be seen again.

Descriptions of the Kraken vary, but it is most commonly depicted as a giant cephalopod, similar to an octopus or squid. Its size is said to be so immense that it could easily be mistaken for an island when seen from a distance. Some accounts even claim that the Kraken's body was over a mile long, with tentacles that could reach up to several miles in length. This monstrous creature was also believed to possess incredible strength, easily crushing ships and creating massive whirlpools that could swallow entire fleets.

The Kraken's fearsome reputation was further cemented by its appearance in various literary works, most notably in the epic poem "The Kraken" by Alfred, Lord Tennyson. In this haunting piece, Tennyson describes the Kraken as a slumbering beast that will one day awaken to herald the end of the world:

"Below the thunders of the upper deep;
Far, far beneath in the abysmal sea,
His ancient, dreamless, uninvaded sleep
The Kraken sleepeth..."

Numerous historical sightings and encounters have also perpetuated the legend of the Kraken. While many of these accounts can likely be attributed to misidentifications of real-life marine creatures, such as giant squids, they have nonetheless contributed to the enduring mystique of this terrifying sea monster.

In modern times, the Kraken has become a popular figure in movies, books, and video games, often symbolizing the unknown and untamed forces of nature. Its fearsome visage and incredible power continue to captivate audiences, reminding them of the ancient myths that have shaped our understanding of the world and its mysteries.

In conclusion, the terrifying Kraken is one of the most iconic and enduring mythical creatures of ancient mythology. Its legend, born from the depths of the ocean and sailors' fears, has transcended time and culture to become a symbol of the awe-inspiring power of nature and the unknown. As we continue to explore the mysteries of our world, the Kraken remains a potent reminder of the ancient tales that have shaped our collective imagination.

The Enduring Legacy of Ancient Mythological Beasts

As we have journeyed through ancient mythology, we have encountered a diverse array of legendary beasts that have captured the imaginations of countless generations. From the mighty Griffin to the terrifying Kraken, these mythical creatures have transcended the boundaries of time and culture, leaving an indelible mark on human history.

The enduring legacy of these ancient mythological beasts can be attributed to their ability to embody the fears, desires, and aspirations of the human spirit. They represent the eternal struggle between good and evil, the quest for knowledge and wisdom, and the pursuit of power and immortality. In many ways, these creatures serve as a mirror, reflecting the complexities and contradictions of the human condition.

Moreover, the stories and legends surrounding these mythical beasts have been a rich source of inspiration for artists, writers, and filmmakers throughout history. From the epic tales of Homer and Ovid to the fantastical worlds of J.R.R. Tolkien and J.K. Rowling, the influence of these ancient creatures can be seen in countless works of literature, art, and cinema. As a result, they have become an integral part of our collective cultural heritage, providing a shared language and symbolism that transcends geographical and temporal boundaries.

In today's modern world, where science and technology have seemingly demystified the mysteries of the universe, the allure of these ancient mythological beasts remains as strong as ever. They continue to captivate our imaginations, reminding us of the power of myth and the enduring appeal of the unknown. As we explore the depths of our creativity and seek to understand the world around us, the legendary beasts of ancient mythology will continue to inspire and enchant us for generations.

In conclusion, the ancient mythological beasts we have explored in this chapter represent a fascinating and diverse tapestry of human imagination and storytelling. Their enduring legacy is a testament to the power of myth and the universal appeal of these timeless tales. As we delve into the unknown and seek to understand the complexities of the human experience, the legendary beasts of ancient mythology will remain a constant source of inspiration, wonder, and awe.

2

ENIGMATIC CREATURES OF EUROPEAN FOLKLORE

An image of a fearsome Kraken emerging from the seas.

Europe, a continent steeped in history and culture, has long been a fertile ground for the birth and evolution of countless myths and legends. From the misty shores of Ireland to the snow-capped peaks of the Alps, the diverse landscapes and ancient civilizations of Europe have given rise to a rich tapestry of folklore that continues to captivate and inspire the imagination of people around the world. At the heart of these tales are the enigmatic creatures that inhabit them, each embodying the fears, hopes, and dreams of the people who brought them to life.

These mythical creatures, both benevolent and malevolent, have played a central role in the oral and written traditions of European cultures for centuries. They have been immortalized in epic poems, ballads, and works of art, serving as cautionary tales, allegories, and symbols of the human experience. They have been passed down through generations, evolving and adapting to the changing world, yet always retaining their core essence and the power to captivate and enchant.

This chapter will delve into the fascinating world of European folklore and explore its most enigmatic creatures. From enchanting Selkies to the alluring Siren, whose deadly song lured sailors to their doom, these mythical beings have captured the imagination of countless generations. We will examine their origins, the stories surrounding them, and their enduring legacy on the collective consciousness of Europe and beyond.

As we embark on this journey through the mythical realms of European folklore, we invite you to suspend disbelief and open your mind to the possibility of a world where the line between reality and fantasy is blurred. The creatures of our wildest dreams and darkest nightmares roam free, for it is in this world that we can truly appreciate the power of storytelling and the enduring allure of the enigmatic creatures that inhabit it.

Please note that other creatures previously discussed that fall into this category include the Kraken (chapter 1) and the Griffin (chapter 1).

The Enchanting Selkies: Shape-Shifting Seal People

In European folklore's vast and diverse world, few creatures capture the imagination quite like the enchanting Selkies. These shape-shifting beings, found predominantly in the legends of Scotland, Ireland, and the Faroe Islands, have long fascinated those who hear their tales. With their unique ability to transform from seals to humans, Selkies have become a symbol of the deep connection between mankind and the natural world and the mysteries that lie beneath the ocean's surface.

Selkies are said to live as seals in the sea, swimming gracefully through the waves and basking on the rocky shores. However, they can shed their seal skins and reveal their true forms when they wish to walk among humans. In their human guise, Selkies are often described as exceptionally beautiful and alluring, with a magnetic charm that is difficult to resist. Moreover, their eyes hold a depth and wisdom that speaks of their ancient origins and the secrets of the deep.

The legends surrounding Selkies are as varied as the waters they inhabit. One of the most famous tales tells of a fisherman who discovers a Selkie's shed skin on the shore. Curious, he takes the skin home with him, only to find a beautiful, naked Selkie woman in his house. With her skin hidden away, the Selkie cannot return to her seal form and is forced to live with the fisherman as his wife. Despite their life together, Selkie's heart remains in the sea, and she longs to return to her true home. Eventually, she discovers the location of her skin and escapes back to the ocean, leaving her human family behind.

This tale, like many others involving Selkies, speaks to the deep longing many people feel for the freedom and mystery of the sea. The Selkie's dual nature represents the duality of human existence – the desire for stability and adventure for both the familiar and the unknown. In this way, the Selkie reminds us of the wild, untamed spirit within us, waiting to be set free.

In addition to their shape-shifting abilities, Selkies are also known for their enchanting voices. They are said to sing hauntingly beautiful songs that can be heard echoing across the waves on quiet nights. These songs are believed to have the power to entrance those who hear them, drawing them into the depths of the sea and the Selkies' watery realm.

With their shape-shifting powers and captivating songs, the enchanting Selkies have left an indelible mark on European folklore. Their tales continue to inspire and captivate those who hear them, reminding them of the deep connection between humans and the natural world and the mysteries that still lie beneath the ocean's surface.

The Elusive Kelpie: The Shape-Shifting Water Horse

The Kelpie, a captivating yet elusive creature, has long been a prominent figure in the folklore of the British Isles, particularly in Scotland and Ireland. This enigmatic being is known for its shape-shifting abilities, often taking the form of a majestic water horse. The Kelpie's mysterious nature and connection to the water have made it a fascinating subject for storytellers and artists, capturing the imagination of generations.

The Kelpie's most well-known form is that of a beautiful, sleek horse with a shimmering, wet mane and a powerful, muscular body. Its eyes are said to be as dark as the deepest loch, and its hooves are often described as being cloven, like those of a goat. The Kelpie is believed to inhabit the rivers, lochs, and streams of the Scottish and Irish countryside, where it uses its enchanting appearance to lure unsuspecting travelers to their doom.

The Kelpie's shape-shifting abilities are not limited to its equine form. It is said that this cunning creature can also take on the appearance of a handsome young man or a beautiful woman, using its charm and allure to entice its victims. However, once the Kelpie has gained the trust of its prey, it will revert to its proper form and drag them beneath the water's surface, where they will meet a tragic end.

Despite its sinister reputation, the Kelpie is not always portrayed as evil. In some tales, it is depicted as a helpful creature, assisting farmers by carrying heavy loads or even helping to grind grain. However, these stories are few and far between, and the Kelpie is more commonly associated with danger and death.

The Kelpie's origins can be traced back to ancient Celtic mythology, where it is believed to have been a symbol of the untamed power of water. The Celts held a deep reverence for the natural world. The Kelpie's association with water, a vital element for life, made it a powerful and respected figure in their mythology.

Over the centuries, the Kelpie has continued to captivate the minds of those who hear its tales. Its enigmatic nature and shape-shifting abilities have made it a popular subject for artists and writers, who have depicted the creature in various forms, from the terrifying to the sublime. The Kelpie's enduring presence in European folklore is a testament to the power of myth and the human imagination as we continue to be drawn to the mysteries of the unknown.

In conclusion, the elusive Kelpie is a fascinating and complex figure in European folklore. Its shape-shifting abilities and connection to the water have made it a popular subject for storytellers and artists alike. Its enduring presence in the mythology of the British Isles is a testament to the power of myth and the human imagination. As we continue to explore the rich tapestry of European folklore, the Kelpie remains an enigmatic and captivating creature, symbolizing the untamed power of the natural world and the mysteries beneath the surface.

The Mischievous Leprechaun: Ireland's Legendary Trickster

With its lush landscapes and rich cultural history, the Emerald Isle has long been a fertile ground for myths and legends. The mischievous leprechaun is among the most famous and enduring of these mythical creatures. This diminutive figure, clad in green and sporting a red beard, has become synonymous with Irish folklore and is often depicted as a playful trickster with a penchant for mischief.

The word "leprechaun" is believed to have originated from the Old Irish word "luchorpán," which translates to "small body." This is a fitting description for these tiny beings, who are said to stand no taller than three feet. Despite their small stature, leprechauns are known for their cunning and intelligence, often using their wits to outsmart humans and other mythical creatures.

Leprechauns are said to be solitary creatures, preferring to live alone and avoid the company of others. They are often depicted as cobblers, crafting exquisite shoes for the fairy folk. This profession is said to be the source of their wealth, as they are rumored to possess a hidden pot of gold. According to legend, if a human is fortunate enough to capture a leprechaun, the creature will grant them three wishes in exchange for its freedom. However, one must be cautious when dealing with these wily beings, as they are notorious for twisting the meaning of wishes to suit their mischievous ends.

The leprechaun's penchant for trickery is not limited to their interactions with humans. They also engage in playful pranks with other mythical creatures, often using their magical powers to create illusions and confusion. However, despite their mischievous nature, leprechauns are not considered malevolent beings. Instead, their tricks are meant to be lighthearted and amusing, reminding them not to take life too seriously.

In addition to their role as tricksters, leprechauns have also been associated with luck and prosperity. This connection is most evident in the famous symbol of the four-leaf clover, which is said to bring good fortune to those who find it. According to legend, leprechauns are drawn to these rare plants and are often found nearby, guarding their pots of gold.

Over the centuries, the image of the leprechaun has evolved and been adapted by various cultures. Today, they are often portrayed as cheerful and benevolent figures, particularly in the context of St. Patrick's Day celebrations. However, the original essence of the leprechaun as a cunning and mischievous trickster remains an integral part of Irish folklore, serving as a reminder of the rich and enigmatic tapestry of European mythology.

The Mysterious Will-o'-the-Wisp: The Deceptive Lights of the Marsh

In the eerie marshlands and bogs of Europe, a curious phenomenon has captivated the imagination of countless generations. Known as the Will-o'-the-Wisp, these enigmatic lights have been the subject of numerous folktales and legends, often portrayed as deceptive spirits or supernatural entities that lure unsuspecting travelers to their doom.

The Will-o'-the-Wisp, also known as ignis fatuus or "foolish fire," appears as a flickering, ghostly light that seems to dance and weave through the darkness of the marshes. These ethereal lights have been described in various colors, ranging from blue and green to yellow and even red. Their elusive nature has made them a source of fascination and fear, as they often lead travelers astray, causing them to become hopelessly lost or even perish in the marsh's treacherous terrain.

In European folklore, the Will-o'-the-Wisp has been attributed to various supernatural beings. In English and Irish mythology, they are often associated with mischievous fairies or spirits who delight in leading humans astray. In some tales, the lights are said to be the souls of the dead, unable to find their way to the afterlife and thus doomed to wander the marshes for eternity. In other stories, the Will-o'-the-Wisp is a nasty creature that seeks to lure travelers to their deaths by drowning in the marsh or leading them into the clutches of other dangerous creatures.

Despite the sinister reputation of the Will-o'-the-Wisp, some legends portray these mysterious lights in a more benevolent light. For example, in certain Scandinavian tales, the lights are believed to be the spirits of helpful elves or dwarves, guiding travelers to safety or revealing hidden treasures. In these stories, the Will o' the-Wisp symbolizes hope and guidance, a beacon of light in the darkness of the marsh.

In reality, the Will-o'-the-Wisp is a natural phenomenon caused by the combustion of gases emitted by decaying organic matter in marshy areas. The most common explanation is that the lights result from phosphine and methane igniting upon contact with oxygen in the air.

This scientific explanation, however, does little to diminish the allure and mystique of the Will-o'-the-Wisp in the popular imagination.

The Mysterious Will-o'-the-Wisp remains an enduring symbol of European folklore's mysterious and otherworldly aspects. These deceptive lights of the marsh remind us of the power of myth and legend to shape our perceptions of the natural world and human fascination with the unknown and the supernatural. As long as the Will-o'-the-Wisp continues to flicker and dance in the darkness of the marsh, it will continue to captivate the minds and imaginations of those who encounter its mysterious glow.

The Terrifying Gorgon: The Deadly Stare of Medusa

In the vast and diverse world of European folklore, few creatures are as terrifying and enigmatic as the Gorgon. The most famous of these fearsome beings is undoubtedly Medusa, synonymous with terror and petrification. With her deadly gaze and hair of writhing serpents, Medusa has captivated the imaginations of storytellers and artists for centuries, leaving an indelible mark on the cultural landscape of Europe.

The Gorgon sisters, Medusa, Stheno, and Euryale, were born to the ancient sea deities Phorcys and Ceto. While Stheno and Euryale were immortal, Medusa was not, making her the most vulnerable of the trio. According to Greek mythology, Medusa was once a beautiful maiden who served as a priestess in the temple of Athena. However, after being seduced by the god Poseidon, the enraged goddess transforms her into a hideous monster. From that moment on, Medusa's once-radiant visage became horrifying, with her golden locks replaced by a nest of venomous snakes.

The mere sight of Medusa's face was said to be so terrifying that it could turn any living creature to stone. This petrifying power made her a formidable foe, and her legend spread far and wide across the lands of Europe. Many brave warriors sought to slay the Gorgon and claim the glory of vanquishing such a fearsome beast, but few succeeded. Finally, the Greek hero Perseus defeated Medusa, using a mirrored shield to avoid her deadly gaze and beheading her with a swift stroke of his sword.

Medusa's severed head retained its petrifying power, and Perseus used it as a weapon in his subsequent adventures. Eventually, he gifted the head to Athena, who affixed it to her shield, the Aegis, as a symbol of her divine protection and power.

The story of Medusa and the Gorgons has been retold and reimagined countless times throughout history, with each new interpretation adding to the rich tapestry of European folklore. From the ancient Greeks to the Romantic poets and beyond, the terrifying figure of Medusa has continued to captivate and inspire. Her image has been immortalized in countless works, from classical sculptures to Renaissance paintings and modern cinema and literature.

The enduring legacy of Medusa and her Gorgon sisters is a testament to the power of myth and the human imagination. These enigmatic creatures of European folklore have transcended the boundaries of time and culture, reminding us of the primal fears that lurk in the shadows of our collective consciousness. As we delve deeper into the world of mythical beasts, we continue to uncover the fascinating stories and legends that have shaped our understanding of the world and our place within it.

The Cunning Basilisk: The King of Serpents

In the vast and diverse realm of European folklore, few creatures are as cunning and feared as the Basilisk. Often referred to as the King of Serpents, this enigmatic creature has captivated the imagination of people for centuries, with tales of its deadly gaze and venomous breath striking terror into the hearts of those who encounter it.

The Basilisk's origins can be traced back to ancient Greece and Rome, where it was believed to be a small, venomous serpent with a lethal gaze. Over time, the legend of the Basilisk evolved, and it became a larger, more formidable creature, often depicted as a serpent with the head of a rooster or a dragon. In some variations of the myth, the Basilisk is said to have the body of a serpent with the head and legs of a rooster, while in others, it is portrayed as a dragon-like creature with a serpent's tail.

Regardless of its physical appearance, the Basilisk's most fearsome attributes are its deadly gaze and venomous breath. It is said that a single glance from the Basilisk can kill a person instantly, turning them to stone or causing them to wither away. In some tales, the Basilisk's gaze is so powerful that it can kill other creatures merely by looking at their reflection in a mirror or a pool of water. Its venomous breath is equally lethal, capable of killing any living being that comes into contact with it.

The Basilisk's cunning nature is often highlighted in the stories that surround it. It is said to be an elusive and intelligent creature, able to outwit its enemies and avoid capture. In some legends, the Basilisk can even understand human speech, allowing it to anticipate the plans of those who seek to destroy it.

Despite its fearsome reputation, the Basilisk is not without its weaknesses. In many tales, the creature is considered vulnerable to the rooster's crowing, which can cause it to die instantly. Additionally, the weasel is often cited as the Basilisk's mortal enemy, as it is immune to the creature's venom and can kill it with a single bite.

The legend of the Basilisk has endured throughout the centuries, inspiring countless works of art, literature, and even modern-day films and television shows. Its cunning nature and deadly abilities have made it a fascinating and terrifying figure in European folklore, reminding us of the power and mystery of the mythical creatures that have captivated our imaginations for generations.

The Alluring Siren: The Deadly Song of the Sea

The enchanting melodies of the Sirens have captivated the minds and hearts of sailors for centuries, luring them to their doom with a song that is as irresistible as it is deadly. As a result, these fascinating creatures of European folklore have become synonymous with temptation and danger, embodying the treacherous beauty of the sea itself.

Originating from ancient Greek mythology, the Sirens were said to be the daughters of the river god Achelous and the muse Melpomene. They were initially depicted as beautiful women with the wings of a bird, allowing them to soar above the waves and enchant sailors with their haunting melodies. Later interpretations of the myth transformed the Sirens into mermaid-like beings, with the upper body of a woman and the tail of a fish, further emphasizing their connection to the sea.

The Sirens' song was said to be so enchanting that no sailor could resist its call. Once they heard the sweet, seductive melody, they would be compelled to steer their ships towards the source of the sound, only to be met with jagged rocks and treacherous waters. Many a ship met its end on the shores of the Sirens' island; their crews were lured to their deaths by the irresistible allure of the song.

The legend of the Sirens has been immortalized in numerous works of literature and art, most notably in Homer's epic poem, The Odyssey. In this tale, the hero Odysseus is warned of the danger the Sirens pose and devises a plan to escape their deadly song. He orders his crew to plug their ears with beeswax while he is tied to the ship's mast, allowing him to hear the Sirens' song without succumbing to its power. As they sail past the island of the Sirens, Odysseus is captivated by their melody but cannot steer the ship toward them, thus saving himself and his crew from certain death.

The Sirens are a powerful symbol of temptation and the dangers of succumbing to one's desires. They represent the seductive power of beauty and the destructive consequences of being lured off course by our passions. In this way, the Sirens are a captivating element of European folklore and a timeless reminder of the perils of temptation and the importance of staying true to one's path.

As we continue to explore the enigmatic creatures of European folklore, we are reminded of the rich tapestry of myths and legends that have shaped our understanding of the world and our place within it. The Sirens, with their haunting song and deadly allure, serve as a testament to the enduring power of these ancient tales and their ability to captivate our imaginations even today.

The Enigmatic Black Dog: The Omen of Death

The enigmatic Black Dog, a spectral hound with glowing red eyes, has haunted the folklore of Europe for centuries. This mysterious creature, often associated with death and misfortune, has been known by various names such as the Barghest in England, the Moddey Dhoo in the Isle of Man, and the Cù Sìth in Scotland. Despite the differences in names and regional variations, the Black Dog remains a chilling and ominous figure in European mythology.

The Black Dog is typically described as a large, black canine with shaggy fur and fiery red or yellow eyes. It is said to be larger than any mortal dog, often the size of a calf or horse. Its appearance is said to be so terrifying that those who encounter it are often left paralyzed with fear. The creature is known to roam the countryside, graveyards, and lonely roads, appearing suddenly and vanishing just as quickly, leaving no trace of its presence.

The origins of the Black Dog legend are difficult to pinpoint, as tales of spectral hounds can be found in various European mythologies. Some scholars believe that the Black Dog may have been inspired by the ancient Celtic belief in the Cù Sìth, a supernatural hound said to be a harbinger of death. Others suggest that the legend may have been influenced by the Norse mythology of the hellhound Garmr, who guarded the entrance to the underworld.

Regardless of its origins, the Black Dog symbolizes death and misfortune in European folklore. It is said that those who encounter the Black Dog are destined to suffer a terrible fate, such as a sudden illness, an accident, or even death itself. In some tales, the Black Dog is said to be a guardian of the spirit world, guiding the souls of the deceased to the afterlife. In others, it is an evil entity that seeks to harm or even kill those who cross its path.

Despite its fearsome reputation, the Black Dog has also been known to serve as a protector in some stories. In these tales, the creature is said to guard lonely travelers against harm, ensuring their safe passage through dangerous or haunted areas. This dual nature of the

Black Dog, both as a harbinger of doom and a guardian spirit, adds to its enigmatic and mysterious allure.

In conclusion, the enigmatic Black Dog remains an enduring and captivating figure in European folklore. Its chilling presence serves as a reminder of the thin veil that separates the world of the living from the realm of the supernatural. The Black Dog's haunting tales continue to captivate the imagination, leaving us to wonder what other mysteries lurk in the shadows of our ancient past.

The Enduring Legacy of European Mythical Creatures

As we have journeyed through the enigmatic world of European folklore, we have encountered a diverse array of mythical creatures that have captured our imaginations and left an indelible mark on our collective consciousness. From enchanting Selkies to the alluring Siren, these legendary beings have not only shaped the stories and traditions of the past but continue to influence our modern world in various ways.

The enduring legacy of these mythical creatures can be seen in numerous aspects of contemporary culture. Literature, art, and film are replete with references and adaptations of these fascinating beings, demonstrating their timeless appeal and power over our imaginations. The Harry Potter series, for instance, draws heavily upon European folklore, incorporating creatures such as the Griffin, the Basilisk, and the Black Dog into its magical world. Similarly, the popular television series Game of Thrones features mythical creatures inspired by European legends, such as the fearsome dragon and the enigmatic White Walkers.

Moreover, these mythical creatures have transcended the realm of fiction and have become deeply ingrained in the cultural identity of the regions from which they originate. The Leprechaun, for example, has become synonymous with Irish culture, while the Kraken is an iconic symbol of Nordic folklore. These creatures are a testament to the rich tapestry of European mythology and the unique characteristics of each region's folklore.

In addition to their cultural significance, the mythical creatures of European folklore also offer valuable insights into the human psyche and our relationship with the natural world. They often embody our deepest fears, desires, and curiosities, reflecting the complexities of human nature and our attempts to make sense of the unknown. For instance, the Kelpie and the Selkie represent our fascination with the mysterious depths of the ocean and our longing to explore its hidden wonders. On the other hand, the Gorgon and the Basilisk symbolize the darker aspects of our psyche, such as our fear of death and the destructive power of our gaze.

Ultimately, the mythical creatures of European folklore serve as a reminder of the power of storytelling and the enduring appeal of the fantastical. They transport us to a world where the boundaries between reality and imagination blur, allowing us to confront our deepest fears and desires in a safe and imaginative space. As we continue to explore the rich tapestry of European mythology, we can draw inspiration from these enigmatic beings and the timeless stories they inhabit, enriching our lives and fostering a deeper appreciation for the diverse cultural heritage that has shaped our world.

3

MYSTICAL MONSTERS OF ASIAN LEGENDS

An image of a cunning nine-tailed fox surrounded by enchantment.

Asia, the largest and most diverse continent on Earth, has long been a cradle of civilization and a melting pot of cultures. From the snow-capped peaks of the Himalayas to the lush jungles of Southeast Asia, the continent has given birth to countless myths, legends, and folktales passed down through generations. These stories, deeply rooted in the rich tapestry of Asian mythology, have shaped the beliefs, values, and identities of the people who call this vast land their home.

One of the most fascinating aspects of Asian mythology is the myriad of mystical monsters and mythical creatures that inhabit its folklore. These beings, often possessing extraordinary powers and abilities, have captivated the imagination of people for centuries. They serve as symbols of the natural world, embodying the fears, hopes, and aspirations of the human spirit. They also act as moral compasses, teaching valuable lessons about the consequences of our actions and the importance of living in harmony with the world around us.

In this chapter, we will journey through the enchanting realm of Asian mythical creatures, exploring the legends and lore surrounding the most captivating and intriguing beings. From the cunning and enchanting Nine-Tailed Fox to the fearsome and powerful Naga, these mystical monsters have left an indelible mark on the collective consciousness of Asia and continue to inspire awe and wonder in the hearts of those who hear their tales.

As we delve into the stories of these mythical creatures, we will uncover the rich cultural heritage that has given rise to their legends. We will also examine how these creatures have evolved, reflecting the changing values and beliefs of the societies that have embraced them. Through this exploration, we hope to shed light on the enduring legacy of Asian mythology and the timeless appeal of its mystical monsters.

So, let us begin our journey into the world of Asian mythical creatures, where the boundaries between the natural and supernatural blur and where the extraordinary becomes an integral part of the fabric of everyday life.

The Nine-Tailed Fox: Cunning and Enchantment

In the vast and diverse realm of Asian mythology, the Nine-Tailed Fox, or Kyubi no Kitsune in Japanese, stands out as one of the most captivating and enigmatic creatures. With its origins in ancient Chinese folklore, the legend of the Nine-Tailed Fox has spread across East Asia, leaving its mark on the mythologies of Japan and Korea. This bewitching creature symbolizes cunning, enchantment, and transformation, embodying the complex and often contradictory nature of the human psyche.

At first glance, the Nine-Tailed Fox appears to be a creature of immense beauty and grace. Its elegant form, adorned with nine luxurious tails, exudes otherworldly charm and allure. However, beneath this enchanting exterior lies a cunning and mischievous spirit capable of using its magical powers to deceive and manipulate those who cross its path. The Nine-Tailed Fox is a master of illusion, able to shape-shift into various forms, including that of a beautiful woman, to seduce and beguile unsuspecting victims.

The tales of the Nine-Tailed Fox are filled with stories of its cunning and guile. In one such tale, the fox transforms into a beautiful woman to seduce a young scholar, only to be exposed by a wise monk who sees through its deception. In another story, the fox takes on the form of a loyal servant to gain the trust of a powerful lord, only to betray him and bring about his downfall. These stories serve as cautionary tales, warning of the dangers of succumbing to temptation and the perils of trusting appearances.

Despite its reputation for cunning and deception, the Nine-Tailed Fox is not an entirely malevolent creature. In some stories, it is portrayed as a benevolent spirit, using its magical powers to help those in need or to protect the innocent from harm. This duality reflects the complex nature of the human psyche, with its capacity for both good and evil, and serves as a reminder that appearances can be deceiving.

The Nine-Tailed Fox has also been associated with spiritual transformation and enlightenment. In many tales, the fox is said to gain a new tail for each century of wisdom and knowledge it acquires, with the ultimate goal of achieving immortality and transcending the mortal realm. This aspect of the legend highlights the importance of wisdom and self-improvement in Asian culture and serves as an allegory for the human quest for enlightenment.

In conclusion, the Nine-Tailed Fox is a fascinating and multifaceted creature that embodies the rich tapestry of Asian mythology. Its tales of cunning, enchantment, and transformation serve as cautionary tales and allegories for the complexities of the human psyche. As a symbol of wisdom and the quest for enlightenment, the Nine-Tailed Fox continues to captivate and inspire, leaving an indelible mark on the cultural landscape of East Asia.

The Nian: A Beast of New Year's Lore

In the vast and diverse world of Asian mythology, the Nian stands out as a unique and captivating creature. This fearsome beast is deeply rooted in Chinese folklore and integral to the country's New Year's celebrations. The Nian's story is not only a thrilling tale of a monstrous creature but also a testament to the resilience and ingenuity of the human spirit.

The Nian, which translates to "year" in Chinese, is said to be a colossal creature with a lion-like appearance, sharp teeth, and a pair of imposing horns. Its body is covered in thick, impenetrable scales, and its eyes gleam with evil intelligence. The Nian is believed to dwell in the ocean's depths or the remote mountains, emerging only once a year during the Spring Festival, also known as the Chinese New Year.

As the legend goes, the Nian would descend upon villages on the eve of the New Year, wreaking havoc and instilling terror in the people's hearts. It would devour livestock, destroy crops, and even snatch away young children from their homes. The villagers, helpless against the might of the Nian, would flee to the mountains to escape its wrath, leaving their homes and livelihoods behind.

However, the tide turned when an old, wise man discovered the Nian's weaknesses. He observed that the creature was frightened by loud noises, bright lights, and the color red. Armed with this knowledge, the villagers devised a plan to ward off the Nian and protect their homes. They adorned their houses with red lanterns and banners, set off deafening firecrackers, and banged on drums and gongs to create a cacophony of sound. The Nian, overwhelmed by the sensory assault, retreated to its lair, and the village was saved.

From that day forward, these customs became integral to the Chinese New Year celebrations. The use of firecrackers, red decorations, and boisterous music and dance serve as festive elements and a symbolic reminder of the triumph over the Nian. The story of the Nian has been passed down through generations. Its influence can be seen in various aspects of Chinese culture, including the traditional lion dance, which is believed to drive away evil spirits and bring good fortune.

The Nian is a fascinating example of how mythology and tradition intertwine to create a rich and enduring cultural narrative. Its story is a testament to the power of unity, courage, and resourcefulness in the face of adversity. As we continue to explore the mystical monsters of Asian legends, the Nian reminds us that even the most fearsome creatures can be overcome through wisdom and determination.

The Qilin: A Symbol of Prosperity and Virtue

In the vast and diverse world of Asian mythology, the Qilin stands out as a symbol of prosperity, virtue, and benevolence. Often referred to as the "Chinese unicorn," this mythical creature is a chimera, combining the features of various animals to create a unique and awe-inspiring being. The Qilin is said to possess the body of a deer, the tail of an ox, the hooves of a horse, and the head of a dragon or lion, adorned with a single horn or a pair of antlers. In addition, its body is covered in brilliantly colored scales, and it is often depicted surrounded by flames or clouds, signifying its divine nature.

The Qilin is believed to have originated in ancient China, with its earliest depictions dating back to the Han Dynasty (206 BCE - 220 CE). Over time, the legend of the Qilin spread throughout Asia, and it became an integral part of the mythologies of Japan, Korea, and Vietnam, known as the Kirin, Girin, and Kỳ Lân, respectively. Despite its appearance and name variations, the Qilin's association with prosperity and virtue remains consistent across these cultures.

One of the most significant aspects of the Qilin is its connection to the arrival of wise and benevolent rulers. It is said that the Qilin only appears during times of peace and prosperity or to herald the birth of a great leader. According to legend, the Qilin appeared to be the mother of Confucius, the great Chinese philosopher, signifying his future impact on the world. Similarly, the Qilin is believed to have appeared before the birth of the legendary Emperor Yao, known for his wisdom and fairness.

In addition to its association with great leaders, the Qilin is known for its gentle and compassionate nature. Despite its fearsome appearance, the Qilin is said to be a vegetarian and is careful not to harm any living creature as it walks upon the earth. It is believed that the Qilin can walk on grass without bending a single blade and even float on water or air, further emphasizing its divine and otherworldly qualities.

The Qilin's benevolent nature is also reflected in its role as a protector of the innocent and a punisher of the wicked. It is said that the Qilin can discern the guilt or innocence of a person and will only punish those who have committed evil deeds. This ability to distinguish between good and evil has made the Qilin popular in art and literature, often representing justice and moral integrity.

In conclusion, the Qilin is a fascinating and complex mythical creature that embodies the virtues of prosperity, wisdom, and benevolence. Its unique appearance and captivating legends have made it an enduring symbol in Asian mythology, reflecting the rich tapestry of beliefs and values that have shaped these ancient cultures. As we continue to explore the world of mythical creatures, the Qilin reminds us of the power of imagination and the timeless appeal of stories that inspire wonder and awe.

The Jiangshi: The Hopping Undead

In the vast and diverse world of Asian mythology, the Jiangshi stands out as one of the most peculiar and intriguing creatures. Hailing from

Chinese folklore, the Jiangshi, also known as the "hopping vampire" or "hopping corpse," is a reanimated corpse that moves by hopping with its arms outstretched. This undead creature is a unique blend of vampire and zombie, combining the thirst for blood with the relentless pursuit of its prey.

The origin of the Jiangshi can be traced back to ancient Chinese beliefs about the soul and the afterlife. According to these beliefs, the soul comprises two parts: the "hun," the spiritual and ethereal aspect, and the "po," which is the corporeal and earthly aspect. When a person dies, the hun leaves the body to ascend to the heavens, while the po remains with the corpse. However, if the po fails to leave the body due to an improper burial or other circumstances, it may reanimate the corpse, creating a Jiangshi.

The appearance of a Jiangshi is both eerie and unsettling. Its skin is typically a shade of green or white, reflecting the decay and decomposition of the corpse. The creature's eyes are wide and lifeless, and its mouth is often twisted into a horrifying grin. The Jiangshi's attire usually consists of traditional Qing Dynasty clothing, reflecting the era in which the legend was most popular.

The Jiangshi's peculiar mode of transportation, hopping, is believed to result from rigor mortis, which stiffens the corpse's limbs and prevents it from walking or running. This hopping motion, combined with the creature's outstretched arms, creates an unnerving and unforgettable image that has haunted the nightmares of generations.

In terms of behavior, the Jiangshi is driven by an insatiable hunger for the life force, or "qi," of living beings. It absorbs this vital energy by touching or breathing on its victims, leaving them weak and lifeless. In some tales, the Jiangshi is also known to consume human blood, similar to the vampires of Western mythology.

Various methods have been devised to protect oneself from the Jiangshi. One common tactic is to place a mirror in front of the creature, as it is believed that the Jiangshi will be frightened by its reflection. Another method involves using a rooster's call, as the crowing of a rooster signifies the arrival of dawn, a time when the undead are forced to retreat. Additionally, religious talismans, inscribed with Daoist symbols, can effectively ward off these hopping horrors.

The Jiangshi has left an indelible mark on Asian folklore and popular culture, appearing in numerous films, novels, and video games. Its unique blend of horror and dark humor, combined with its distinctively unsettling appearance, ensures that the Jiangshi will continue to captivate and terrify audiences for generations.

The Garuda: The Majestic Bird-God

The Garuda, a majestic and powerful bird god, soars high in Asian mythology, casting a spellbinding presence across various cultures. With its roots in Hindu and Buddhist traditions, the Garuda has captivated the imagination of countless generations, symbolizing strength, wisdom, and divine protection. This awe-inspiring creature is a fascinating mythical being and a testament to the rich tapestry of Asian legends.

The Garuda's physical appearance is a striking blend of human and avian features. Often depicted with the body of a strong, golden-feathered bird and the head, arms, and torso of a man, the Garuda exudes an aura of regality and might. Its wings, which are said to span miles, create gusts of wind powerful enough to uproot trees and send mountains tumbling. The Garuda's piercing gaze is believed to penetrate the deepest secrets, while its sharp beak and talons can defeat even the most formidable foes.

In Hindu mythology, the Garuda is revered as the mount of Lord Vishnu, one of the principal deities responsible for preserving the universe. The Garuda's unwavering loyalty and devotion to Vishnu are legendary, and it is often depicted carrying the god on its back as they traverse the cosmos. The Garuda's role as Vishnu's mount signifies its status as a symbol of divine authority and protection and its ability to transport the deity to different realms and dimensions.

The Garuda's mythical origins are steeped in tales of valor and triumph. According to Hindu lore, the Garuda was born from the cosmic egg laid by the sage Kashyapa's wife, Vinata. Upon hatching, the

Garuda embarked on a perilous quest to rescue his mother from the clutches of her rival, Kadru, the mother of serpents. The Garuda's epic battle against the serpents and his ultimate victory cemented his status as a symbol of courage and perseverance.

In the Buddhist tradition, the Garuda is regarded as a guardian of the Buddhist teachings, or dharma. Therefore, it is often depicted in the company of other mythical creatures, such as the dragon, the phoenix, and the lion, each representing different aspects of the dharma. The Garuda's association with wisdom and spiritual insight is further emphasized by its role as a protector of sacred texts and relics.

The Garuda's influence extends beyond mythology and religion, permeating various aspects of Asian culture. As a result, it is a prominent symbol in the iconography of several Asian countries, including Indonesia, Thailand, and India. The Garuda's image adorns temples, palaces, and monuments, constantly reminding them of its enduring legacy.

In conclusion, the Garuda is a majestic and awe-inspiring mythical creature that embodies the essence of Asian mythology. Its tales of courage, loyalty, and wisdom continue to captivate the hearts and minds of those who encounter it. As a symbol of divine protection and spiritual insight, the Garuda is a testament to the rich and diverse tapestry of Asian legends, soaring high above the annals of time.

The Rakshasa: Demons of Ancient India

The Rakshasa, a fearsome and malevolent creature, has long been a staple of Indian mythology. These demonic beings are often depicted as shape-shifting, bloodthirsty monsters with a penchant for causing chaos and destruction. Their origins can be traced back to the ancient Hindu scriptures, where they are described as the offspring of the deity Brahma. Over time, the Rakshasa have become an integral part of Indian folklore, capturing the imagination of storytellers and audiences alike.

Rakshasas are typically portrayed as grotesque, with sharp fangs, bulging eyes, and a hulking physique. Their skin color ranges from dark shades of blue and green to pitch black, further emphasizing their sinister nature. Despite their monstrous appearance, Rakshasas can shape-shift, allowing them to assume any form they desire. This power enables them to deceive and manipulate unsuspecting victims, often leading to their untimely demise.

The Rakshasa are known for their insatiable hunger for human flesh, which they consume with great relish. They are also said to possess immense strength and magical powers, making them formidable adversaries. In many tales, they are depicted as using their supernatural abilities to terrorize and torment humans, often for their amusement. However, it is important to note that not all Rakshasas are inherently evil. Some stories feature benevolent Rakshasas who use their powers for the greater good, protecting humans from harm and assisting them in their quests.

One of the most famous Rakshasas in Indian mythology is Ravana, the primary antagonist of the Hindu epic Ramayana. Ravana, a ten-headed Rakshasa king, is known for his immense power, cunning intellect, and mastery of magic. His abduction of Sita, the wife of the hero Rama, sets the stage for an epic battle between the forces of good and evil. Ravana's defeat at Rama's hands is a powerful reminder of the triumph of righteousness over wickedness.

The Rakshasa also features prominently in the Mahabharata, another ancient Indian epic. They are portrayed as skilled warriors and powerful sorcerers who often conflict with the story's heroes. The epic's protagonist, Arjuna, encounters several Rakshasas during his adventures, including the fearsome Bakasura, whom he ultimately vanquishes.

In conclusion, the Rakshasa is a fascinating and complex aspect of Indian mythology. These demonic beings embody the darker aspects of human nature, serving as a cautionary reminder of the consequences of succumbing to our baser instincts. Yet, at the same time, their shape-shifting abilities and supernatural powers have captivated the imaginations of countless generations, ensuring their enduring presence in the rich tapestry of Asian legends.

The Kappa: The Mischievous River Imp

The Kappa, a captivating and mischievous creature, has long been a prominent figure in the folklore of Japan. Known for their impish behavior and unique appearance, these river imps have captured the imagination of generations, serving as both a cautionary tale and a source of fascination. In this section, we will delve into the world of the Kappa, exploring their physical characteristics, role in Japanese mythology, and the lessons they impart.

At first glance, the Kappa is an odd amalgamation of various animals. With the body of a child-sized turtle, a frog's limbs, and a bird's beak, the Kappa's appearance is nothing short of peculiar. However, their most distinctive feature is the small, water-filled depression atop their heads, known as the "sara." This shallow bowl is the source of the Kappa's power, and should the water ever spill or evaporate, the creature would lose its strength and be rendered helpless.

The Kappa are known to inhabit the rivers and ponds of Japan, where they engage in a variety of mischievous activities. While some of their antics are relatively harmless, such as playing pranks on unsuspecting humans or challenging them to games of skill, other behaviors are far more sinister. The Kappa have been known to drown animals and humans, dragging them beneath the water's surface and feasting on their entrails. It is said that the Kappa is particularly fond of a mythical ball called the "shirikodama," which is believed to reside within the human body and grant its possessor immense power.

Despite their malevolent tendencies, the Kappa is not entirely devoid of redeeming qualities. They are known to possess a strong sense of honor and are bound by the rules of etiquette. One such rule dictates that if a person were to bow before a Kappa, the creature would be compelled to return the gesture, causing the water in its sara to spill and rendering it powerless. In this weakened state, the Kappa can be easily defeated or forced to promise never to harm the individual again. Additionally, the Kappa are said to possess vast knowledge of medicine and are known to share this wisdom with humans in exchange for their freedom or offerings of food.

The tales of the Kappa serve as a reminder of the importance of respecting the natural world and its inhabitants. While the Kappa may be mischievous and, at times, dangerous, they also embody the complexities of nature, which can be both nurturing and destructive. By understanding and respecting the Kappa, we can learn to coexist with the many wonders and mysteries of the natural world.

In conclusion, the Kappa is a fascinating and multifaceted aspect of Asian mythology. Their unique appearance, mischievous behavior, and complex moral code provide a captivating glimpse into the rich tapestry of Japanese folklore. As we continue to explore the mystical monsters of Asian legends, the Kappa stands as a testament to the enduring power of myth and the lessons it can teach us about our world and ourselves.

The Aswang: Shape-Shifting Predators of the Philippines

In the vast and diverse world of Asian mythology, the Aswang holds a unique and terrifying place in the folklore of the Philippines. Known as one of the region's most feared and evil creatures, the Aswang is a shape-shifting predator that has haunted the nightmares of Filipinos for centuries. This enigmatic creature is a master of deception, capable of transforming into various forms to stalk its prey and instill terror in the hearts of those who encounter it.

The Aswang is often described as a nocturnal creature, hiding in the shadows and emerging only under the cover of darkness. It is said to be able to change its appearance at will, taking on the guise of animals such as dogs, cats, or even pigs. In some tales, the Aswang can also assume human form, blending seamlessly into society and making it nearly impossible to identify them among ordinary people.

Despite their shape-shifting abilities, Aswangs are not without their distinguishing features. In their true form, they are said to have long, sharp claws, leathery wings, and a long, whip-like tongue. This tongue is used to suck the blood or consume their victims' internal organs, typically unborn fetuses, infants, or the sick and elderly. The Aswang's preference for the most vulnerable members of society has made them a symbol of pure evil and a source of great fear for many Filipinos.

As with many mythical creatures, the origins of the Aswang can be traced back to ancient beliefs and superstitions. Some scholars suggest that the Aswang myth may have been influenced by the arrival of Spanish colonizers, who brought tales of witches and vampires. Others believe that the Aswang manifests the anxieties and fears that have plagued human societies for generations, particularly the fear of the unknown and the dangers that lurk in the shadows.

The Aswang has also played a significant role in Filipino popular culture, appearing in numerous films, television shows, and books. These portrayals often emphasize the creature's shape-shifting abilities and insatiable appetite for human flesh, reinforcing the Aswang's status as a symbol of terror and evil.

In conclusion, the Aswang is a fascinating and fearsome creature that has captivated the imaginations of Filipinos for centuries. Its shape-shifting abilities and predilection for preying on the most vulnerable members of society have made it a potent symbol of evil and a fixture in the rich tapestry of Asian mythology. As the Aswang continues to haunt the nightmares of those who hear its tale, it serves as a chilling reminder of the power of folklore and the enduring nature of our deepest fears.

The Naga: Serpents of Wisdom and Power

The Naga, a mythical serpent, is significant in the folklore and mythology of various Asian cultures. These magnificent beings are often depicted as colossal, multi-headed snakes or half-human, half-serpent beings. The Naga are revered for their wisdom, power, and vital role in the balance of the natural world.

The origins of the Naga can be traced back to ancient Indian mythology, where they were considered the children of the great serpent Ananta, who serves as the bed of the Hindu god Vishnu. However, over time, the Naga's influence spread across Asia, and they became an integral part of the mythologies of countries such as Cambodia, Thailand, and Indonesia.

In Hinduism, the Naga are associated with the underworld, known as Patala, where they reside in magnificent palaces filled with unimaginable treasures. They are also believed to be the guardians of sacred texts and esoteric knowledge. In addition, the Naga are often depicted as the protectors of the gods, and their presence is believed to bring good fortune and prosperity.

In Buddhism, the Naga are considered to be powerful and wise beings who possess the ability to transform into human form. They are often portrayed as the protectors of the Buddha and the Dharma, the teachings of Buddhism. One of the most famous stories involving the Naga is that of Mucalinda, a serpent king who protected the Buddha from the elements as he meditated under the Bodhi tree.

The Naga also play a significant role in the folklore of Southeast Asia, where they are believed to be the guardians of water sources, such as rivers, lakes, and seas. In these cultures, the Naga are often associated with rain and fertility, as their movements are believed to cause the monsoon rains that nourish the land. The Naga are also believed to have the power to control the weather and are often invoked in rituals to bring about favorable conditions for agriculture.

In many Asian cultures, the Naga are considered to be both benevolent and malevolent beings. While revered for their wisdom and power, they are also feared for their ability to bring about natural disasters, such as floods and droughts. The Naga are often depicted as fiercely protective of their territory, and those who disrespect or harm their domain may face their wrath.

Despite their fearsome reputation, the Naga continues to be a symbol of wisdom, power, and the balance of nature in Asian mythology. Their enduring presence in the legends and folklore of the region serves as a reminder of the deep connection between humans and the natural world, as well as the importance of respecting and preserving the delicate balance between all living beings.

In conclusion, the Naga is a fascinating and complex mythical creature that has captivated people's imaginations across Asia for centuries.

Their dual nature as both wise protectors and fearsome adversaries is a powerful reminder of the delicate balance within the natural world and the importance of respecting and preserving this balance for future generations.

The Tengu: The Mysterious Mountain Spirits

The Tengu, enigmatic mountain spirits of Japanese folklore, have captivated the imagination of generations with their unique blend of mystique, wisdom, and mischief. These elusive beings are often depicted as humanoid creatures with avian features, such as beaks or wings, and are believed to possess supernatural powers. The Tengu are both revered and feared, as they are known to be protectors of the natural world and martial arts teachers, yet they are also notorious for their trickery and penchant for causing chaos.

The Tengu's origins can be traced back to ancient Chinese mythology, where they were initially depicted as dog-like demons. Over time, as the legend of the Tengu spread to Japan, their appearance evolved to incorporate bird-like characteristics, drawing inspiration from the Chinese mythological creature, the Triangle. The Tengu's association with the mountains is believed to have been influenced by the Shugendō religion, which emphasizes the spiritual power of nature and the importance of ascetic practices in the wilderness.

There are two primary types of Tengu in Japanese folklore: the Karasu-Tengu (crow Tengu) and the Yamabushi Tengu (mountain priest Tengu). The Karasu-Tengu are characterized by their crow-like appearance, black wings, and beaks and are considered the lesser of the two types. They are often portrayed as mischievous tricksters, delighting in causing human confusion and chaos.

The Yamabushi Tengu, on the other hand, are depicted as more human-like, with long noses and flowing robes. They are believed to be the spirits of deceased mountain priests who have attained supernatural powers through their ascetic practices. These Tengu are revered as wise teachers and protectors of the mountains and are often sought out by those seeking to learn the secrets of martial arts or gain spiritual enlightenment.

The Tengu have played a significant role in Japanese culture, appearing in various art, literature, and theater forms. They are often portrayed as antagonists and protagonists, reflecting their dual nature as protectors and tricksters. In some stories, the Tengu are depicted as benevolent guardians who aid humans in their quest for knowledge or justice, while in others, they are portrayed as malevolent beings who use their powers to deceive and manipulate.

The Tengu's association with martial arts has also made them popular figures in Japanese martial arts, with many schools claiming to have been founded by Tengu or attributing their techniques to the teachings of these mysterious mountain spirits.

The Tengu's enigmatic nature and ability to embody wisdom and mischief have made them enduring figures in the realm of Asian mythical creatures. They serve as a reminder of the dual nature of existence, where light and darkness, good and evil, are inextricably intertwined. The Tengu continues to captivate the imagination of those who encounter their legend, inviting us to explore the mysteries of the natural world and the depths of our inner selves.

The Enduring Legacy of Asian Mythical Creatures

As we have journeyed through the mystical realms of Asian legends, we have encountered a diverse and fascinating array of mythical creatures. From the cunning Nine-Tailed Fox to the majestic Garuda, these beings have captured the imaginations of countless generations, leaving an indelible mark on the cultural fabric of the region. The enduring legacy of these mythical creatures is a testament to the power of storytelling and the human desire to explore the unknown.

One of the most striking aspects of these mythical creatures is how they embody the values, fears, and aspirations of the societies that created them. The Qilin, for example, symbolizes prosperity and virtue, reflecting the importance of these qualities in Chinese culture. Similarly, the Nian, a beast that terrorizes villages during the Lunar New Year, represents the challenges and uncertainties people face daily.

These mythical creatures also serve as a means of connecting with the natural world and the forces that govern it. For example, the Naga, revered as serpents of wisdom and power, is believed to control the waters and bring fertility to the land. On the other hand, the Kappa are mischievous river imps that remind us of the unpredictable and sometimes dangerous nature of water. By personifying these elements, these creatures help us make sense of the world and our place within it.

Moreover, the stories of these mythical creatures often contain moral lessons and cautionary tales. For example, the Rakshasa, demons of ancient India, warn against the dangers of greed and corruption, while the Aswang, shape-shifting predators of the Philippines, reminds us of the potential for evil that lies within each of us. Engaging with these narratives encourages us to reflect on our actions and strive to be better individuals.

In conclusion, the mythical creatures of Asian legends continue to captivate and inspire us, offering a window into the rich tapestry of human imagination. As we share these stories with future generations, we preserve the region's cultural heritage and foster a deeper understanding of the human experience. Through the tales of these mystical monsters, we are reminded of the power of storytelling to shape our world, challenge our beliefs, and, ultimately, bring us closer together.

4

FEARSOME BEINGS OF AFRICAN MYTHOLOGY

An image of the Grootslang, a mythical giant serpent-elephant hybrid.

Africa, the cradle of humanity, is a continent rich in history, culture, and mythology. Its diverse landscape, encompassing vast deserts, lush rainforests, and expansive savannas, has given rise to countless tales of mythical creatures and fearsome beings. These stories passed down through generations, have not only entertained but also served as cautionary tales, moral lessons, and explanations for the mysteries of the natural world.

African mythology is as diverse as the continent itself, with each region and ethnic group boasting its unique pantheon of gods, spirits, and supernatural beings. While some entities are benevolent or helpful to humans, others are decidedly more sinister. These fearsome beings, often born from the darkest corners of the human imagination, have captivated and terrified audiences for centuries.

In this chapter, we will delve into African mythology and explore the most fearsome beings that have haunted the dreams and stories of countless generations. From the colossal Grootslang, a monstrous serpent-elephant hybrid, to the malevolent Tokoloshe, a mischievous and malicious dwarf, these creatures embody the fears and anxieties of the people who brought them to life.

We will also encounter the shape-shifting Adze, a vampire-like being that preys on the unsuspecting; the Ninki Nanka, a dragon-like swamp dweller with a taste for human flesh; and the Bouda, a were-hyena shapeshifter that stalks the night. The skies are not safe either, as the Impundulu, a lightning bird of doom, soars above while the enchanting Mami Wata lures unsuspecting victims into her watery domain.

The terrifying Popobawa, a bat-like creature that terrorizes communities, shares the stage with the Yumboes, silver-haired spirits of the forest, and the Kongamato, a prehistoric flying terror that has been sighted in modern times. Each of these fearsome beings has its unique story, reflecting the rich tapestry of African mythology and the enduring power of the human imagination.

As we journey through this dark and fascinating realm, we will learn about the creatures themselves and the cultural context in which they were created. By understanding the fears and beliefs that gave rise to these mythical beings, we can better appreciate the rich and diverse world of African mythology and the enduring legacy of Africa's fearsome beings. So, let us embark on this thrilling adventure and uncover the mysteries of these legendary creatures that have captivated the hearts and minds of people for centuries.

The Grootslang: The Giant Serpent-Elephant Hybrid

In African mythology's vast and diverse realm, one of the most fearsome and awe-inspiring creatures is the Grootslang, a colossal hybrid of a serpent and an elephant. This legendary beast is said to dwell in Africa's deep caves and rivers, particularly in the Richtersveld region of South Africa. The Grootslang, which translates to "big snake" in Afrikaans, is a formidable force of nature, possessing the cunning intelligence of an elephant and the lethal power of a serpent.

According to ancient African folklore, the Grootslang was one of the first creatures to roam the earth, created by the gods. However, the gods soon realized they had made a grave mistake by imbuing the Grootslang with immense strength and intellect. To rectify their error, they split the creature into two separate beings: the elephant and the snake. But, as the story goes, one Grootslang managed to escape this divine intervention, and this lone survivor has continued to terrorize the African landscape ever since.

The Grootslang is often depicted as a massive serpent with the head of an elephant, complete with enormous tusks and a long, powerful trunk. Its body is covered in thick, impenetrable scales, and its eyes are said to glow with a sinister, otherworldly light. The Grootslang is a master of stealth and ambush, using its serpentine body to silently slither through the underbrush and strike its prey with lightning speed.

The Grootslang is known to be a highly territorial creature, fiercely guarding its lair and the surrounding area from any intruders. It is said to have a particular affinity for precious gems and metals, hoarding vast treasures within its subterranean domain. Many a brave adventurer has been lured by the promise of untold riches, only to meet their doom at the hands (or rather, the coils) of the Grootslang.

Despite its fearsome reputation, the Grootslang is not without its weaknesses. According to some legends, the creature can be outwitted by those who possess great cunning and intelligence. In one such tale, a clever hunter managed to trick the Grootslang into releasing him from its deadly embrace by offering it a valuable gemstone in exchange for his life. The Grootslang, unable to resist the allure of the precious stone, agreed to the bargain and spared the hunter's life.

The Grootslang is a powerful symbol of the African wilderness's untamed and often perilous beauty. It is a testament to the rich and diverse tapestry of African mythology, which continues to captivate and inspire the imaginations of people worldwide. As we delve deeper into the fearsome beings of African mythology, we will encounter even more fascinating and terrifying creatures that have shaped the continent's cultural heritage.

The Tokoloshe: The Mischievous and Malicious Dwarf

In African mythology's vast and diverse realm, the Tokoloshe stands out as one of the most intriguing and enigmatic figures. This small, impish creature is a staple in the folklore of various African cultures, particularly among the Zulu, Xhosa, and Sotho peoples of southern Africa. The Tokoloshe, also known as Tikoloshe or Hili, is a mischievous, sometimes malevolent dwarf-like being believed to possess supernatural powers. Despite its diminutive stature, the Tokoloshe is a force to be reckoned with, as it is known to wreak havoc in the lives of those who cross its path.

The physical appearance of the Tokoloshe is as fascinating as its mythical reputation. Often described as a small, hairy humanoid creature with a gremlin-like face, the Tokoloshe is said to have disproportionally long arms and legs and a single buttock. Its most striking feature, however, is its large, prominent eyes that are believed to possess a hypnotic power capable of inducing fear and submission in its victims.

The Tokoloshe is notorious for its mischievous nature, often playing pranks on unsuspecting humans. However, its antics can quickly escalate from harmless mischief to more sinister acts, such as causing illness, stealing livestock, or even bringing death to those who have angered it. Furthermore, it is said that the Tokoloshe can become invisible at will, allowing it to move about undetected and carry out its nefarious deeds.

In African folklore, the Tokoloshe is often summoned by evil individuals, such as witches or sorcerers, to do their bidding and inflict harm upon their enemies. As a result, people in these cultures have developed various rituals and talismans to protect themselves from the Tokoloshe's wrath. One common practice is to raise their beds on bricks, as it is believed that the Tokoloshe cannot climb and reach those who sleep at a higher elevation. Others may place protective charms around their homes or consult with traditional healers to ward off the creature's evil influence.

Despite its fearsome reputation, the Tokoloshe also serves as a cautionary figure in African folklore, reminding people of the consequences of engaging in malicious acts or dabbling in dark magic. The tales of the Tokoloshe's exploits are passed down through generations, serving as entertainment and a warning to those tempted to stray from the path of righteousness.

In conclusion, the Tokoloshe is a captivating and complex figure in African mythology, embodying both the mischievous and malevolent aspects of the supernatural world. Its enduring presence in the folklore of various African cultures is a testament to the power of myth and the human imagination and a reflection of the universal fascination with the mysterious and the unknown.

The Adze: The Shape-Shifting Vampire

In African mythology's vast and diverse realm, the Adze stands out as one of the most fearsome and enigmatic creatures. Hailing from the Ewe people of Ghana and Togo, the Adze is a shape-shifting vampire that has haunted the nightmares of generations. This sinister being is known for its cunning, hostility, and insatiable thirst for human blood.

The Adze is a master of disguise, able to transform itself into various forms to deceive and prey upon its victims. In its natural state, the Adze is a small, innocuous insect, often resembling a firefly. This allows it to move undetected through the night, seeking its next unsuspecting target. However, when ready to strike, the Adze undergoes a terrifying transformation, morphing into a humanoid figure with sharp claws, elongated limbs, and a grotesque, distorted face.

The Adze's primary source of sustenance is human blood, which it consumes with a voracious appetite. It is particularly drawn to the blood of children, who it believes possess a purer and more potent life force. To obtain this precious resource, the Adze employs its shape-shifting abilities to infiltrate homes, often entering through small openings such as keyholes or cracks in the walls. Once inside, it reverts to its humanoid form and uses its razor-sharp claws to pierce the skin of its sleeping victims, draining their blood and leaving them weak and vulnerable.

In addition to its bloodthirsty nature, the Adze is also known for its evil influence on the minds of its victims. Those targeted by the Adze often experience vivid nightmares, hallucinations, and a general sense of unease. Some even believe the Adze can possess individuals, driving them to commit heinous acts against their will.

Despite its fearsome reputation, the Adze is not invulnerable. Like many creatures of myth, it is susceptible to certain rituals and talismans that can ward off its evil presence. The Ewe people have developed a variety of protective measures to keep the Adze at bay, including charms, amulets, and incantations. Additionally, the Adze is said to be repelled by the scent of certain herbs and spices, which can be used to create a barrier around one's home.

The Adze serves as a chilling reminder of the darker aspects of African mythology, embodying the primal fears of the unknown and the dangers that lurk in the shadows. Its shape-shifting abilities and insatiable hunger for human blood make it a formidable adversary that has haunted the collective imagination of the Ewe people for centuries.

As we continue to explore the fearsome beings of African mythology, the Adze stands as a testament to the power of folklore and the enduring allure of the supernatural.

The Ninki Nanka: The Dragon-Like Swamp Dweller

The Ninki Nanka is a fearsome creature that has long haunted the swamps and wetlands of West Africa, particularly in countries such as Gambia, Senegal, and Guinea-Bissau. This mythical being is often described as a dragon-like creature with a long, serpentine body, a crocodile-like head, and large, sharp teeth. Its size is immense, with some claiming it to be as long as 30 feet or more. The Ninki Nanka is believed to dwell in the murky depths of swamps, rivers, and other bodies of water, emerging only to terrorize and devour unsuspecting victims.

The legend of the Ninki Nanka has been passed down through generations, with many local tribes attributing the creature's existence to ancient folklore and superstition. Some believe that the Ninki Nanka is a guardian of the swamps, protecting the delicate balance of the ecosystem and punishing those who dare to disturb it. Others view the creature as a malevolent force, a harbinger of death and destruction that preys upon the weak and vulnerable.

Despite its fearsome reputation, encounters with the Ninki Nanka are rare. Those who claim to have seen the creature often describe it as a terrifying sight, with its massive body slithering through the water and its eyes glowing with an eerie, supernatural light. Some accounts even suggest that the Ninki Nanka can hypnotize its prey, luring them into the water before dragging them beneath the surface to meet their doom.

The Ninki Nanka has become a symbol of the unknown and the mysterious in African mythology, a reminder of the dangers that lurk in the shadows and the power of the natural world. Yet, while many dismiss the creature as a myth, others continue to believe in its existence, sharing stories of close encounters and narrow escapes. Whether fact or fiction, the Ninki Nanka remains a captivating figure in the pantheon of Africa's fearsome beings, a chilling reminder of the ancient and primal forces that continue to shape the continent's rich and diverse mythology.

The Bouda: The Werehyena Shapeshifter

In African mythology's vast and diverse realm, the Bouda stands out as one of the most fearsome and enigmatic creatures. Also known as the Werehyena, this shapeshifter has captivated the imagination of countless generations with its cunning, ferocity, and insatiable hunger. In this section, we will delve into the origins, characteristics, and cultural significance of the Bouda, exploring the reasons behind its enduring appeal and the lessons it imparts.

The Bouda is primarily found in the folklore of East Africa, particularly in Ethiopia and Somalia. It is believed to be a human who possesses the supernatural ability to transform into a hyena, either at will or under the influence of a full moon. This transformation is often accompanied by gruesome rituals, including consuming human flesh and the desecration of graves. In some accounts, the Bouda is portrayed as a sorcerer or witch who uses their powers for evil purposes. In contrast, in others, it is depicted as a cursed individual forced to endure their monstrous condition as a form of divine punishment.

The physical appearance of the Bouda in its hyena form is both awe-inspiring and terrifying. It is typically described as a massive, muscular beast with a hulking frame, razor-sharp claws, and a powerful jaw capable of easily crushing bones. In addition, its eyes are said to glow with an eerie, supernatural light, and its fur is often depicted as being mottled and unkempt, reflecting its sinister nature. In its human form, the Bouda is said to be virtually indistinguishable from ordinary people, allowing it to blend seamlessly into society and prey upon unsuspecting victims.

The Bouda's fearsome reputation is further enhanced by its cunning and intelligence. It is said to be a master of deception, capable of luring its victims into a false sense of security before striking with lethal force. In some tales, the Bouda can even mimic human speech and adopt the appearance of a loved one, making it an even more formidable adversary. Its insatiable appetite for human flesh is matched only by the relentless pursuit of its prey, making it a symbol of the darker aspects of human nature and the dangers that lurk beneath the surface of seemingly ordinary individuals.

The cultural significance of the Bouda is multifaceted and complex. On the one hand, it serves as a cautionary tale about the perils of succumbing to one's baser instincts and the consequences of indulging in immoral behavior. On the other hand, it also represents the fear of the unknown and the ever-present threat of hidden dangers in a world of uncertainty and chaos. The Bouda's ability to shapeshift and blend into human society serves as a metaphor for the dual nature of humanity, highlighting the potential for both good and evil within each of us.

In conclusion, the Bouda, or Werehyena, is a fascinating and fearsome being that has captured the imagination of countless generations in African mythology. Its unique combination of physical prowess, cunning, and supernatural abilities make it a formidable creature that continues to inspire awe and terror in equal measure. As a symbol of the darker aspects of human nature and the hidden dangers that lurk beneath our everyday lives, the Bouda is a powerful reminder of the complexities and contradictions that define our existence.

The Impundulu: The Lightning Bird of Doom

In the vast and diverse realm of African mythology, the Impundulu, also known as the Lightning Bird, stands out as one of the most fearsome and awe-inspiring creatures. This enigmatic being is deeply rooted in the folklore and belief systems of various tribes across southern Africa, including the Zulu, Xhosa, and Pondo people. The Impundulu symbolizes power, destruction, and the untamed forces of nature. Its presence in the myths and legends of Africa reminds us of the mysterious and often terrifying aspects of the world around us.

The Impundulu is said to be a massive bird, often described as being the size of a human or even larger. Its appearance is a striking combination of various bird species, with an eagle's sharp beak, a hawk's powerful talons, and the peacock's iridescent plumage.

However, the Impundulu's most distinctive feature is its ability to summon and control lightning and thunderstorms. As it soars through the sky, it is often accompanied by dark clouds, fierce winds, and brilliant flashes of lightning, striking fear into the hearts of those who witness its flight.

The origins of the Impundulu are shrouded in mystery, with some legends suggesting that it is a supernatural being created by the gods, while others claim that it is a powerful spirit summoned by witches and sorcerers. Regardless of its origins, the Impundulu is believed to possess immense power, and its presence is often seen as an omen of impending doom or disaster. In some stories, the Lightning Bird is said to be a servant of powerful witches who use its abilities to wreak havoc on their enemies and bring misfortune to those who have wronged them.

The Impundulu is not only feared for its control over the elements but also for its insatiable appetite for human blood. It is said to be a vampiric creature that feeds on the life force of its victims, leaving them weak and drained of energy. In some tales, the Impundulu can shapeshift into a handsome young man, using its charm and good looks to seduce unsuspecting women and lure them to their doom.

Despite its fearsome reputation, the Impundulu is not without its weaknesses. According to some legends, the Lightning Bird can be defeated by a brave and skilled warrior, who must strike the creature with a weapon made of metal, as this is the only material capable of piercing its supernatural hide. In other stories, the Impundulu can be outwitted or tricked into revealing its true nature, allowing its enemies to gain the upper hand and vanquish the creature.

The Impundulu, or Lightning Bird of Doom, is a fascinating and terrifying figure in African mythology, embodying the destructive power of nature and the darker aspects of the human psyche. Its presence in the myths and legends of Africa serves as a reminder of the complex and often frightening world that exists beyond the boundaries of our understanding and the enduring power of the stories passed down through generations to entertain and inspire.

The Mami Wata: The Enchanting Water Spirit

The Mami Wata, a captivating and enigmatic figure in African mythology, is a water spirit that has captivated the hearts and minds of people across the continent for centuries. Often depicted as a beautiful woman with a fishtail or serpentine lower body, the Mami Wata symbolizes the beauty and danger found in the depths of Africa's rivers, lakes, and oceans.

The name "Mami Wata" is derived from the pidgin English phrase "Mammy Water," which itself is a translation of the African term for "Mother Water." This name reflects the Mami Wata's role as a nurturing and protective figure and her connection to the life-giving properties of water. In many African cultures, water is considered a sacred element, and the Mami Wata is often seen as a guardian of this vital resource.

The Mami Wata is a complex and multifaceted figure, embodying both the seductive allure and the treacherous nature of water. She is often portrayed as a stunningly beautiful woman with long, flowing hair and enchanting eyes that can enter anyone who gazes at her. Her lower body may be that of a fish, a snake, or even a crocodile, symbolizing her connection to the mysterious depths of the water and the creatures that dwell within it.

In many African myths, the Mami Wata tempts unsuspecting men to their doom with her irresistible beauty. She may appear near the water's edge to a fisherman or traveler, beckoning them to join her in the depths. But, unfortunately, those who fall under her spell are often never seen again, either drowned by the powerful currents or spirited away to her underwater realm.

However, the Mami Wata is not always a malevolent figure. In some stories, she is a benevolent spirit who grants boons to those who honor her and respect the sanctity of the water. She may bestow wealth, fertility, or healing upon those who pay homage to her, and she is sometimes invoked as a protector against waterborne diseases and other dangers.

The Mami Wata's dual nature as a seductive temptress and a nurturing mother figure reflects the complex relationship many

African cultures have with water. On the one hand, water is a vital resource that sustains life and provides nourishment; on the other hand, it can be a dangerous and unpredictable force that can bring destruction and death. The Mami Wata embodies this duality, reminding us of the power and mystery of the water surrounding us.

In conclusion, the Mami Wata is a fascinating and enigmatic figure in African mythology, representing the beauty and danger of the continent's waterways. Her enduring appeal and the wide variety of stories surrounding her serve as a testament to the deep connection that African cultures have with the natural world and the powerful forces that shape it.

The Popobawa: The Terrifying Bat-Like Creature

In the vast and diverse realm of African mythology, the Popobawa stands out as one of the most fearsome and terrifying creatures. Originating from the East African island of Zanzibar, the Popobawa is a bat-like creature that has struck fear into the hearts of locals for generations. Its name, derived from the Swahili words "popo" (bat) and "bawa" (wing), aptly describes its monstrous appearance. With its massive wingspan, sharp talons, and piercing red eyes, the Popobawa is a creature that is not easily forgotten.

The legend of the Popobawa dates back to the 1960s when it was first reported to have terrorized the people of Zanzibar. Since then, sightings and encounters with this fearsome being have continued to be reported, particularly during political unrest or upheaval. The Popobawa is said to be a shape-shifter, able to take on the form of both humans and animals, making it difficult to identify and even more challenging to escape.

The Popobawa is known for its nocturnal habits, stalking its victims under darkness. It is said to target individuals who are alone, often attacking them in their own homes. The creature is believed to possess supernatural strength, allowing it to overpower its victims quickly. Once it has subdued its prey, the Popobawa is said to feed on their fear, drawing energy from their terror and leaving them in utter panic.

What makes the Popobawa particularly terrifying is its ability to induce mass hysteria. Reports of sightings or encounters with the creature often lead to widespread panic, with entire communities gripped by fear. This fear is so potent that it is believed to attract the Popobawa, causing it to target those who are most afraid. As a result, the legend of the Popobawa has become a self-perpetuating cycle of terror.

Despite numerous attempts to capture or kill the Popobawa, the creature has remained elusive, adding to its mystique and the fear it instills in those who believe in its existence. Some have suggested that the Popobawa manifests collective anxiety, a symbol of the fears and uncertainties plaguing the human psyche. Others maintain that the creature is a very real and malevolent force, a reminder of the dark and mysterious forces that lurk in the shadows of our world.

Regardless of its true nature, the Popobawa remains an enduring figure in African mythology, a testament to the power of fear and the human imagination. As long as people continue to whisper its name in hushed tones and share stories of its terrifying exploits, the legend of the Popobawa will continue to haunt the nightmares of those who dwell in its shadow.

The Yumboes: The Silver-Haired Spirits of the Forest

Deep within Africa's lush, verdant forests, a mysterious and enchanting race of beings is said to dwell. Known as the Yumboes, these elusive creatures have captivated the imaginations of generations, leaving a lasting impression on the rich tapestry of African mythology. Often described as ethereal and otherworldly, the Yumboes are a fascinating example of the fearsome beings that populate the continent's folklore.

Standing at a mere two feet tall, the Yumboes are diminutive in stature but possess an undeniable presence. Their most striking feature is their long, flowing silver hair, which shimmers and dances in the dappled sunlight of their forest home. Their skin is said to be as pale as moonlight, and their eyes sparkle like the stars in the night sky. Despite their small size, the Yumboes are known for their agility and grace, moving through the trees with the elegance of a ballet dancer.

The Yumboes are often compared to the fairies and sprites of European folklore, as they share many similarities in appearance and behavior. They are known to be mischievous and playful, delighting in playing tricks on unsuspecting humans who venture too far into their territory. However, their pranks are rarely malicious and generally regarded as benevolent spirits who protect the forest and its inhabitants.

One of the most intriguing aspects of the Yumboes is their connection to the natural world. They are said to be the guardians of the forest, ensuring that the ecosystem's delicate balance is maintained. They are particularly fond of the animals that share their home, and they are known to communicate with them in a language understood only by the wild creatures.

The Yumboes are also believed to possess magical powers, which they use to maintain the harmony of their environment. For example, they can control the elements, summoning rain to nourish the plants and commanding the wind to carry away any threats. They are also said to be able to heal the sick and injured, using their knowledge of the forest's medicinal plants to create potent remedies.

Despite their fearsome reputation, encounters with the Yumboes are rare, as they are known to be shy and elusive creatures. They prefer to remain hidden from the prying eyes of humans, only revealing themselves to those who have earned their trust. However, those fortunate enough to meet a Yumboe often speak of the experience with awe and wonder, describing the creatures as captivating in their beauty.

In conclusion, the Yumboes are a fascinating and unique addition to African mythology's pantheon of fearsome beings. Their ethereal beauty and magical powers have captured the imaginations of generations, and their role as guardians of the forest serves as a reminder of the importance of respecting and preserving the natural world. As we continue to explore Africa's rich and diverse mythology, the Yumboes stand as a testament to the enduring power of folklore and the human imagination.

The Kongamato: The Prehistoric Flying Terror

Deep within the heart of Africa's vast and mysterious wilderness, legends speak of a terrifying creature that soars through the skies, striking fear into those who dare to venture into its domain. Known as the Kongamato, this prehistoric flying terror has captivated the imagination of locals and explorers, leaving a lasting impression on the continent's rich tapestry of myths and folklore.

The Kongamato, which translates to "breaker of boats" or "overwhelmer of boats" in the Kaonde language, is said to inhabit the swamps and rivers of Zambia, Angola, and the Democratic Republic of Congo. Described as a large, pterosaur-like creature with a wingspan of up to seven feet, the Kongamato is believed to be a relic of the prehistoric era, a living fossil that has managed to survive the test of time.

With its leathery wings, sharp beak, and formidable size, the Kongamato is a force to be reckoned with. According to local legends, this fearsome creature is known to attack small boats and canoes, capsizing them and leaving their occupants at the mercy of the treacherous waters. Some accounts even suggest that the Kongamato is responsible for the mysterious disappearances of fishermen and travelers who have ventured too close to its territory.

The first recorded encounter with the Kongamato dates back to the early 20th century when British explorer Frank H. Melland documented his experiences with the creature in his book, "In Witchbound Africa." Melland described the Kongamato as a monstrous, bat-like creature with a four to seven feet wingspan and a beak with razor-sharp teeth. He also noted that the locals were terrified of the creature and would often carry charms and amulets to ward off its malevolent presence.

Since then, numerous sightings and encounters with the Kongamato have been reported, fueling speculation and debate among cryptozoologists and enthusiasts. Some believe that the Kongamato is a surviving species of pterosaur, while others argue that it could be a large, unknown species of bat or bird. On the other hand, Skeptics dismiss the Kongamato as a mere figment of the imagination, a product of superstition and fear.

Regardless of its true nature, the Kongamato remains an enduring symbol of Africa's rich and diverse mythology. As a fearsome being that has captured the imagination of generations, the Kongamato serves as a reminder of the continent's vast and untamed wilderness, where ancient legends and modern-day mysteries continue to coexist in the shadows of the unknown.

The Enduring Legacy of Africa's Fearsome Beings

As we have journeyed through the diverse and captivating world of African mythology, we have encountered many fearsome beings that have captured our imaginations and sent shivers down our spines. From the colossal Grootslang to the mischievous Tokoloshe, these mythical creatures have played a significant role in shaping the cultural identity and folklore of the African continent.

The enduring legacy of Africa's fearsome beings can be attributed to their ability to embody the fears, hopes, and beliefs of the people who have passed down these tales through generations. These creatures serve as cautionary tales, teaching valuable lessons about the dangers of the natural world, the importance of respecting the unknown, and the consequences of one's actions.

Moreover, these fearsome beings have transcended the boundaries of folklore and have found their way into modern popular culture. They have inspired countless works of art, literature, and film, allowing their stories to reach a global audience and further solidifying their place in the annals of mythology.

The rich tapestry of African mythology, woven with the threads of these fearsome beings, is a testament to the power of storytelling and the human imagination. These creatures have not only shaped the cultural landscape of Africa but have also left an indelible mark on the collective consciousness of people worldwide.

As we conclude our exploration of Africa's fearsome beings, we must recognize the importance of preserving these stories and passing them down to future generations. By doing so, we ensure that the legacy of these mythical creatures and the lessons they impart will continue to thrive, inspiring awe and wonder in the hearts and minds of those who encounter them.

In the end, the fearsome beings of African mythology remind us of the vast and diverse world that exists beyond our own experiences. They challenge us to confront our fears, embrace the unknown, and appreciate the beauty and complexity of the world around us. And as long as these stories continue to be told, the fearsome beings of African mythology will continue to captivate, terrify, and inspire us all.

5

FANTASTICAL CREATURES OF THE AMERICAS

An image of the Thunderbird, a powerful symbol in Native American lore.

The Americas, a vast and diverse landmass stretching from the Arctic tundra to the southernmost tip of Argentina, has long been a fertile ground for the imagination. For thousands of years, the indigenous peoples of this vast territory have woven intricate tapestries of myth and legend, giving birth to a myriad of fantastical creatures that continue to captivate and inspire us today. These mythical beings, often deeply rooted in the natural world and the spiritual beliefs of their creators, serve as a testament to the rich cultural heritage of the Americas and the boundless creativity of the human mind.

In this chapter, we will embark on a thrilling journey through the mythical landscapes of the Americas, exploring the stories and legends that surround some of the most fascinating and enigmatic creatures ever conceived. From the powerful Thunderbird, a symbol of Native American lore, to the terrifying Wendigo, a cannibalistic spirit of the North, we will delve into the origins, characteristics, and cultural significance of these captivating beings.

As we venture further south, we will encounter the mysterious Chupacabra, a bloodsucking creature that has terrorized Latin America for decades, and the shape-shifting sorcerers known as Skinwalkers, who have haunted the Navajo people for generations. We will also meet the mischievous Pukwudgie, the little people of Wampanoag folklore, and the awe-inspiring Quetzalcoatl, the feathered serpent deity of Mesoamerican mythology.

Our journey will take us deep into the forests of North America, where the enigmatic Sasquatch is said to roam, and to the haunted shores of Mexico, where the weeping woman known as La Llorona is believed to wander in search of her lost children. We will also explore the legends of the Cadejo, the dueling canine spirits of Central America, and the fearsome Jersey Devil, a beast that has stalked the Pine Barrens of New Jersey for centuries.

Throughout this exploration, we will uncover the fascinating stories behind these mythical creatures and examine the enduring legacy they have left on the cultures and traditions of the Americas. By delving into the rich tapestry of myth and legend that has shaped the continent, we will gain a deeper understanding of the human experience and the power of storytelling to connect us to our past, present, and future. So, let us begin our journey into the realm of the fantastical creatures of the Americas and prepare to be amazed, frightened, and inspired by the wonders that await us.

The Thunderbird: A Powerful Symbol of Native American Lore

The Thunderbird, a majestic and awe-inspiring creature, has long been a prominent figure in the mythology and folklore of various Native American tribes. This enormous bird, often depicted with a wingspan that stretches across the sky, is said to possess immense power and control over the elements, particularly thunder, and lightning. The Thunderbird's significance in Native American lore is due to its physical prowess and its spiritual symbolism, as it represents the forces of nature and the balance between the earthly and spiritual realms.

The Thunderbird myth's origin varies among tribes, but a common theme is its role as a protector and guardian of the people. In some legends, the Thunderbird is considered a divine being sent by the Creator to watch over the earth and its inhabitants. It is said to soar high above the clouds, watching the world below and intervening when necessary to maintain harmony and balance.

One of the most well-known stories involving the Thunderbird comes from the Ojibwe tribe. In their lore, the Thunderbird is locked in an eternal battle with the Great Horned Serpent, an evil creature that dwells in the ocean's depths and threatens to consume the world. The Thunderbird, with its mighty wings and powerful talons, fights to keep the serpent at bay, protecting the people from its destructive influence. This epic struggle between the forces of good and evil is a recurring theme in many Native American myths. It serves as a reminder of the delicate balance in the natural world.

The Thunderbird's association with thunder and lightning is another key aspect of its mythology. It is believed that the beating of its enormous wings creates the sound of thunder, while the lightning streaks across the sky result from the sparks generated by its eyes or beak. Some tribes even attribute the formation of storms to the Thunderbird, as it is said to bring rain and life-giving water to the earth.

In addition to its role as a protector and guardian, the Thunderbird is also seen as a symbol of strength, courage, and wisdom. Its image has been used in various forms of Native American art, including totem poles, masks, and ceremonial regalia, to invoke its power and protection. The Thunderbird's presence in these artistic expressions serves as a reminder of the deep connection between the Native American people and the natural world and the spiritual forces that govern it.

In conclusion, the Thunderbird is a powerful and enduring symbol in Native American lore, representing the awe-inspiring forces of nature and the spiritual connection between the people and their environment. Its presence in various myths and legends is a testament to the rich cultural heritage of the Native American tribes and their deep understanding of the world around them. As we continue to explore the fascinating realm of mythical creatures, the Thunderbird stands as a reminder of the importance of respecting and preserving the delicate balance of our natural world.

The Wendigo: The Terrifying Cannibalistic Spirit of the North

The Wendigo, a horrifying creature that has haunted the nightmares of the indigenous peoples of North America for centuries, is a chilling example of the darker side of mythology. This terrifying, cannibalistic spirit is said to roam the cold, desolate forests of the northern United States and Canada, preying on the weak and vulnerable. The Wendigo symbolizes the harshness of nature and the dangers of isolation and is a cautionary tale about the consequences of indulging in one's darkest desires.

The Wendigo is often described as a gaunt, skeletal figure with sunken eyes and a ravenous hunger for human flesh. Its appearance reflects its insatiable appetite, as it is never satisfied and always on the hunt for its next meal. In addition, the creature is believed to possess supernatural strength, speed, and endurance, making it a formidable predator that is nearly impossible to escape.

The origins of the Wendigo legend can be traced back to the Algonquian-speaking tribes of North America, such as the Ojibwe, Cree, and Innu. These tribes shared a common belief in the existence of malevolent spirits that could possess and corrupt the minds of humans, driving them to commit unspeakable acts of violence and depravity. The Wendigo was one such spirit, particularly feared for its ability to turn ordinary people into ravenous cannibals.

The Wendigo was said to be born from the darkest depths of human desperation. According to legend, when a person was driven to the brink of starvation and resorted to cannibalism to survive, they would become possessed by the spirit of the Wendigo. This transformation would strip them of their humanity, leaving behind a monstrous creature driven solely by its insatiable hunger for human flesh.

The Wendigo myth served as a powerful deterrent against cannibalism, which was considered a serious taboo among the indigenous peoples of North America. However, the fear of becoming a Wendigo was so deeply ingrained in their culture that it persisted despite extreme hunger and deprivation. This fear was not entirely unfounded, as there have been numerous historical accounts of Wendigo sightings and encounters, particularly during famine and hardship.

In addition to its role as a cautionary tale, the Wendigo legend also serves as a metaphor for the destructive power of greed and selfishness. The creature's insatiable hunger reflects the human tendency to consume and exploit resources without regard for the consequences. The Wendigo is a stark reminder of the potential for the darkness within each of us and the importance of maintaining a balance between our desires and the needs of others.

The Wendigo may be a terrifying figure of myth and legend, but its enduring presence in the folklore of the Americas is a testament to the power of storytelling and the human imagination. Through the chilling tale of the Wendigo, we are reminded of the importance of respecting the natural world, the delicate balance between life and death, and the consequences of giving in to our darkest desires.

The Chupacabra: The Mysterious Bloodsucking Creature of Latin America

The Chupacabra, a name that sends shivers down the spines of many Latin Americans, is a creature that has captivated the imagination of people across the region for decades. The name "Chupacabra" is derived from the Spanish words "chupar," meaning "to suck," and "cabra," meaning "goat." This fearsome creature is said to be a blood-sucking beast that preys on livestock, particularly goats, leaving behind a trail of lifeless carcasses drained of their blood.

First reported in Puerto Rico in the mid-1990s, the Chupacabra has since been sighted in various countries across Latin America, including Mexico, Chile, and Argentina. The creature is often described as around 3 to 4 feet tall, with a humanoid appearance, sharp claws, and glowing red eyes. Some accounts depict the Chupacabra as having a row of sharp spines running down its back, while others describe it as having leathery, bat-like wings.

The Chupacabra's modus operandi is as terrifying as its appearance. It is said to attack its prey in the dead of night, puncturing the neck of its victim with its razor-sharp fangs and draining the blood until the animal is left lifeless. Farmers have reported finding their livestock with mysterious puncture wounds, completely drained of blood, fueling the legend of this elusive creature.

Skeptics argue that the Chupacabra is nothing more than a product of mass hysteria fueled by the fear of the unknown and the power of suggestion. They point to the lack of concrete evidence, such as clear photographs or physical remains, as proof that the creature is a figment of the imagination. In addition, some experts have suggested that the livestock deaths attributed to the Chupacabra could be the work of wild dogs or other predators, while others believe that the phenomenon may result from a rare disease affecting the animals.

Despite the skepticism, the legend of the Chupacabra continues to thrive in Latin American culture. The creature symbolizes the region's rich folklore, inspiring countless stories, songs, and even movies. The

Chupacabra has also found its way into popular culture worldwide, with references to television shows, books, and video games.

In conclusion, the Chupacabra remains one of Latin America's most enigmatic and terrifying mythical creatures. Its bloodsucking habits and eerie appearance have captured the imagination of people across the region and beyond, leaving many to wonder whether this elusive beast lurks in the night's shadows. Whether the Chupacabra is a genuine cryptid or simply a product of folklore and fear, its legend endures as a chilling reminder of the mysteries still hidden within the depths of the Americas.

The Skinwalker: The Shape-Shifting Sorcerers of Navajo Legend

The vast, arid landscapes of the American Southwest have long been home to the Navajo people, whose rich cultural heritage is steeped in ancient legends and folklore. Among the most chilling and enigmatic of these tales are those of the Skinwalkers, shape-shifting sorcerers who are said to possess the power to transform into animals and manipulate the world around them. These sinister beings have been a source of fascination and terror for generations. Their stories continue to captivate those who seek to unravel the mysteries of the Navajo's supernatural world.

According to Navajo legend, Skinwalkers, or "yee naaldlooshii" in the Navajo language, are individuals who have attained the highest level of witchcraft, known as the "Witchery Way." This dark and malevolent practice is said to grant its practitioners the ability to assume the form of various animals, such as coyotes, wolves, bears, and birds of prey. To achieve this transformation, the Skinwalker must don the skin of the animal they wish to become, a gruesome act believed to imbue them with the creature's strength, agility, and cunning.

However, the Skinwalker's powers extend far beyond their shape-shifting abilities. These nefarious sorcerers are also said to possess a range of supernatural abilities, including mind control, telepathy, and the power to inflict illness and misfortune upon their victims. They are often depicted as malevolent tricksters, using their powers to sow chaos and discord within their communities. Some stories even suggest that Skinwalkers can control the weather, summoning storms and other natural disasters to wreak havoc on those who have incurred their wrath.

The origins of the Skinwalker legend are shrouded in mystery, with many Navajo people reluctant to discuss these terrifying beings for fear of attracting their attention. However, it is widely believed that the Skinwalker's powers are derived from a perversion of traditional Navajo healing practices, with the sorcerer harnessing the spiritual energy of the universe for their nefarious purposes. This corruption of sacred knowledge is considered a grave offense within Navajo culture. As a result, those suspected of practicing the Witchery Way are often ostracized and feared by their communities.

Despite the secrecy surrounding the Skinwalker legend, stories of these shape-shifting sorcerers have spread far beyond the boundaries of the Navajo Nation, capturing the imagination of those drawn to the darker side of American folklore. Tales of eerie encounters with these elusive beings have been reported throughout the Southwest, with many witnesses describing terrifying encounters with creatures that defy nature's laws. While skeptics may dismiss these accounts as mere superstition, the enduring power of the Skinwalker legend serves as a testament to the deep-rooted fears and beliefs that continue to shape the cultural landscape of the Americas.

In conclusion, the Skinwalker is a chilling and enigmatic figure in Navajo legend, embodying the darker aspects of human nature and the supernatural world. As a shape-shifting sorcerer with a range of terrifying powers, the Skinwalker is a potent reminder of the dangers that can arise when sacred knowledge is twisted and corrupted for personal gain. As we delve deeper into the fantastical creatures of the Americas, the Skinwalker stands as a haunting symbol of the complex and often frightening tapestry of myths and legends that define the region's rich cultural heritage.

The Pukwudgie: The Mischievous Little People of Wampanoag Folklore

The Pukwudgie, a fascinating and enigmatic creature, has long been a part of the Wampanoag folklore, a Native American tribe from the northeastern region of the United States. These mythical beings are often described as small, humanoid creatures, standing about two to three feet tall, with a distinctive appearance sets them apart from other mythical beings. They are said to have smooth, grey skin, large ears, noses, and fingers that end in sharp talons. Their most striking feature, however, is the porcupine-like quills that adorn their backs, which they can use as weapons by shooting at their enemies.

The Pukwudgie is known for its mischievous and sometimes malevolent nature. They possess various magical abilities, including the power to shape-shift, control fire, and even cast spells. While they are often portrayed as tricksters, playing harmless pranks on unsuspecting humans, they can also be dangerous when provoked or crossed. There are numerous tales of Pukwudgies luring people to their deaths by leading them off cliffs or into treacherous swamps.

Despite their small stature and seemingly playful demeanor, the Pukwudgie should not be underestimated. They are known to be fiercely independent and harbor deep resentment towards humans. This animosity is believed to stem from an ancient conflict between the Pukwudgies and the Wampanoag people, in which the tribe's hero, Maushop, drove the creatures away from their lands. Since then, the Pukwudgies have been seeking revenge, often targeting humans who venture too close to their territory.

The Pukwudgie's presence in Wampanoag folklore serves as a reminder of the complex relationship between humans and the natural world. These creatures embody nature's unpredictable and sometimes dangerous aspects, as well as the importance of respecting the boundaries between the human and the supernatural realms. The Pukwudgie's enduring presence in the folklore of the Americas is a testament to the power of storytelling and the human imagination, as well as the rich cultural heritage of the Wampanoag people.

In conclusion, the Pukwudgie is a captivating and intriguing mythical creature that has captured the imagination of generations. As a symbol of nature's unpredictable and sometimes perilous aspects, the Pukwudgie serves as a reminder of the importance of respecting the boundaries between the human and supernatural realms. The tales of these mischievous little people continue to be passed down through the generations, ensuring that the legacy of the Americas' mythical creatures remains alive and well.

The Quetzalcoatl: The Feathered Serpent Deity of Mesoamerican Mythology

The Quetzalcoatl, a captivating and enigmatic figure, is one of the most prominent and revered deities in the pantheon of Mesoamerican mythology. This fascinating creature, often depicted as a feathered serpent, has captivated the imagination of countless generations and continues to be a symbol of the region's rich cultural heritage.

The name "Quetzalcoatl" is derived from the Nahuatl language, spoken by the Aztecs and other indigenous peoples of Mexico. It combines two words: "quetzal," a brightly colored bird native to Central America, and "coatl," which means serpent. This unique fusion of bird and snake represents the duality of the deity, embodying both the celestial and the earthly realms.

Various Mesoamerican cultures worshiped Quetzalcoatl, including the Aztecs, the Toltecs, and the Maya. Although the attributes and legends associated with the deity may vary slightly among these cultures, Quetzalcoatl is consistently portrayed as a powerful and benevolent figure. He is often associated with the wind, the dawn, and the planet Venus, as well as being the patron of learning, agriculture, and the arts.

One of the most famous legends surrounding Quetzalcoatl is the story of his role in the creation of humanity. According to Aztec mythology, the world had been created and destroyed four times before the current era, known as the Fifth Sun. In this era, Quetzalcoatl descended to the underworld, Mictlan, to retrieve the bones of the previous generations of humans. With the help of his twin brother, Xolotl, he collected the bones and brought them back to the surface. Quetzalcoatl then mixed the bones with his blood, giving birth to the human race.

Another popular tale recounts Quetzalcoatl's role in introducing maize, a staple crop in Mesoamerican societies. In this story, the feathered serpent discovered maize hidden away in a mountain by the gods. Recognizing the potential benefits of this crop for humanity, Quetzalcoatl transformed himself into an ant and infiltrated the mountain, retrieving a single kernel of maize. He then shared this precious gift with the people, teaching them how to cultivate and harvest the crop, thus ensuring their survival and prosperity.

Throughout history, the figure of Quetzalcoatl has been the subject of various interpretations and speculations. Some scholars believe that the deity may have been inspired by an actual historical figure, a wise and benevolent ruler who was later deified. Others suggest that the myth of Quetzalcoatl may have been influenced by contact with other cultures, such as the ancient Chinese, who also revered a dragon-like creature.

Regardless of its origins, the legend of Quetzalcoatl remains an integral part of the cultural fabric of the Americas. The feathered serpent deity continues to inspire awe and wonder, serving as a testament to the rich and diverse mythological traditions of the Mesoamerican people.

The Sasquatch: The Enigmatic Giant Hominid of North American Forests

The Sasquatch, also known as Bigfoot, is one of the most iconic and enigmatic mythical creatures of the Americas. This elusive giant hominid is said to inhabit the dense forests of North America, particularly in the Pacific Northwest region of the United States and Canada. The Sasquatch has captured the imagination of countless individuals, with numerous sightings, footprints, and even alleged photographs and videos fueling the ongoing debate about its existence.

The name "Sasquatch" is derived from the Halkomelem word

"sásq'ets," a term used by the indigenous Salish people of British Columbia to describe a large, hairy, ape-like creature. The more popular moniker, "Bigfoot," was coined in the late 1950s after a series of giant footprints were discovered in Northern California. These footprints, measuring up to 24 inches in length, sparked widespread interest in the creature and led to an explosion of reported sightings and encounters.

Descriptions of the Sasquatch vary, but most accounts depict it as a massive, bipedal creature standing between 6 and 10 feet tall, covered in thick, dark hair. It is often said to possess a strong, unpleasant odor and to emit eerie, high-pitched vocalizations. Some witnesses have reported seeing the creature walking on all fours, while others claim to have observed it using tools or exhibiting human-like intelligence.

The Sasquatch has deep roots in the folklore and oral traditions of various indigenous tribes across North America. Many of these stories describe the creature as a powerful, supernatural being who can communicate with humans and even shape-shift. Some tribes view the Sasquatch as a guardian of the forest, while others regard it as an evil entity to be feared and avoided.

Skeptics argue that the Sasquatch is nothing more than a product of human imagination, fueled by misidentifications of known animals, such as bears or large primates, and perpetuated by hoaxes and tall tales. Yet, despite the lack of concrete evidence, the search for the elusive creature continues, with dedicated researchers and enthusiasts employing modern technology and scientific methods to prove the existence of the Sasquatch.

The enduring fascination with the Sasquatch can be attributed to the human desire to explore the unknown and uncover the natural world's mysteries. The idea that a massive, undiscovered primate could be roaming the forests of North America challenges our understanding of the world and ignites our curiosity. Whether the Sasquatch is a genuine undiscovered species or simply a captivating myth, its place in the pantheon of the Americas' mythical creatures is secure. Its legend will continue to captivate the minds of generations to come.

The La Llorona: The Weeping Woman of Mexican Folklore

The La Llorona, or "The Weeping Woman," is a chilling figure in Mexican folklore whose haunting wails have echoed through the ages. This tragic figure is said to be the spirit of a woman who drowned her children in a river in a fit of jealousy and rage. Overcome with grief and remorse, she is now cursed to wander the earth, weeping and searching for her lost children for all eternity.

The origins of the La Llorona legend can be traced back to the Spanish conquest of Mexico. However, the story has evolved over the centuries, incorporating elements of indigenous mythology and Spanish folklore. Today, the tale of La Llorona is a cautionary tale that warns against the dangers of jealousy, betrayal, and the consequences of one's actions.

According to the legend, La Llorona was once a beautiful woman named Maria who lived in a small village. She fell in love with a wealthy man, and they had two children together. However, her lover eventually grew tired of her and left her for another woman. In a fit of jealousy and despair, Maria took her children to the river and drowned them. When she realized the horror of what she had done, she also threw herself into the river, hoping to join her children in death.

However, Maria was cursed to wander the earth as La Llorona instead of finding peace in the afterlife. Her spirit is said to haunt rivers and lakes, dressed in a white gown with long, flowing black hair. She can be heard weeping and wailing, crying out for her lost children. Those who hear her cries are said to be marked for misfortune or even death.

Over the years, the story of La Llorona has been adapted and retold in various forms, including literature, film, and music. The legend has also become a popular subject for artists, who often depict her as a beautiful but tragic figure, forever mourning her lost children.

In contemporary Mexican culture, the tale of La Llorona warns children to stay away from rivers and lakes lest the Weeping Woman snatch them away. Parents often use the story to teach their children the importance of obedience and the consequences of their actions.

The legend of La Llorona is a powerful reminder of the enduring nature of folklore and how stories can be used to teach important lessons and preserve cultural traditions. As one of the most well-known and chilling tales from the Americas, the story of the Weeping Woman continues to captivate and terrify audiences, ensuring that her mournful cries will echo through the ages.

The Cadejo: The Dueling Canine Spirits of Central American Legends

The rich tapestry of Central American folklore is home to many mythical creatures, each with unique stories and characteristics. The Cadejo stands out as a captivating and enigmatic figure among these fascinating beings. The Cadejo is a supernatural entity that takes the form of a large, shaggy canine, often appearing to travelers during the night. However, the Cadejo is not just one creature but two opposing spirits – one benevolent and the other malevolent – locked in an eternal struggle for the souls of those they encounter.

The White Cadejo, or "Cadejo Blanco," is a guardian spirit, a symbol of protection and guidance. It is said to have a luminous white coat, shining eyes, and a gentle demeanor. The White Cadejo appears to lost or weary travelers, guiding them safely to their destinations and warding off potential dangers lurking in the shadows. Many believe the White Cadejo is an angelic being sent by the divine to watch over and protect those in need.

In stark contrast, the Black Cadejo, or "Cadejo Negro," is a nasty and fearsome creature. Its fur is as dark as night, its eyes glow red with malice, and the stench of death and decay often accompanies its presence. The Black Cadejo is said to prey on vulnerable travelers, seeking to lead them astray and ultimately claim their souls. Some legends suggest that the Black Cadejo is a demonic entity, while others believe it to be the restless spirit of a cursed individual, forever bound to wander the earth in its monstrous form.

The duality of the Cadejo is a recurring theme in Central American folklore, representing the eternal struggle between good and evil, light and darkness. The Cadejo's dual nature serves as a reminder that life is a journey filled with choices and that the path one chooses to follow can have profound consequences.

In many tales, the White and Black Cadejo are said to confront one another, engaging in fierce battles for the fate of the souls they encounter. These clashes are physical and symbolic, as the Cadejo embodies the internal struggles that each individual must face in their own life. The outcome of these battles is often left uncertain, emphasizing the importance of personal choice and the power of free will.

The Cadejo's enduring presence in Central American legends is a testament to the region's rich cultural heritage and the universal appeal of stories that explore the complexities of human nature. The Cadejo's tale is one of mystery, intrigue, and the eternal struggle between good and evil – a captivating narrative that continues to resonate with audiences across generations.

The Jersey Devil: The Fearsome Beast of the Pine Barrens

Nestled within the dense forests of southern New Jersey lies a region shrouded in mystery and fear: the Pine Barrens. This vast expanse of land, characterized by its sandy soil and thick vegetation, is home to one of American folklore's most chilling and enigmatic creatures - the Jersey Devil. For centuries, tales of this fearsome beast have haunted the imaginations of those who dwell near the Pine Barrens, and its legend continues to captivate the minds of people across the nation.

The origins of the Jersey Devil can be traced back to the early 18th century, when Mother Leeds, a resident of the Pine Barrens, was said to have given birth to her 13th child. According to the legend, Mother Leeds, overwhelmed by the prospect of raising yet another child, cursed her unborn baby, exclaiming, "Let this one be a devil!" To her horror, her wish was granted. Upon its birth, the child transformed into a grotesque creature with the head of a goat, the wings of a bat, and the body of a kangaroo. The beast let out a blood-curdling scream, then attacked its family before escaping through the chimney and disappearing into the darkness of the Pine Barrens.

Since that fateful night, countless sightings of the Jersey Devil have been reported throughout the region. Descriptions of the creature vary, but most accounts depict it as a monstrous, bipedal being with a piercing shriek and glowing red eyes. Some believe that the Jersey Devil possesses supernatural abilities, such as the power to teleport or manipulate the elements. Others claim it is a harbinger of doom, appearing only to those about to meet a tragic end.

Over the years, the Jersey Devil has become a symbol of fear and fascination for the people of New Jersey and beyond. Its legend has inspired numerous books, films, and television shows, and a professional hockey team is named in its honor. Despite numerous attempts to capture or debunk the creature, the Jersey Devil remains an enigma, lurking in the shadows of the Pine Barrens and haunting the dreams of those who dare to venture too close.

In conclusion, the Jersey Devil is a prime example of the rich and diverse tapestry of mythical creatures that inhabit the Americas. Its enduring legacy serves as a testament to the power of folklore and the human imagination and a reminder of the mysteries that still lie hidden within the depths of our vast and varied continent.

The Enduring Legacy of the Americas' Mythical Creatures

As we reach the end of our journey through the fantastical creatures of the Americas, we must reflect on the enduring legacy these mythical beings have left on the cultures and societies that have birthed them. From the powerful Thunderbird to the enigmatic Sasquatch, these creatures have captivated the imaginations of generations, transcending time and space to become integral parts of the collective consciousness.

The stories and legends surrounding these mythical creatures testify to the rich tapestry of human imagination and our innate desire to understand the world around us. They provide a window into the fears, hopes, and beliefs of the people who have lived on this vast and diverse continent. In addition, these creatures have been used to explain natural phenomena, teach moral lessons, and provide a sense of identity and belonging to various communities.

These mythical creatures' enduring legacy is evident in how they continue to permeate popular culture today. They have inspired countless works of art, literature, and film, capturing the hearts and minds of audiences worldwide. From the terrifying Wendigo to the mischievous Pukwudgie, these creatures have become iconic symbols that continue to captivate and intrigue.

Moreover, studying these mythical creatures offers valuable insights into the cultural and historical contexts from which they emerged. By examining the origins and evolution of these legends, we can gain a deeper understanding of the societies that created them and the values they held dear. In this way, the fantastical creatures of the Americas serve as a bridge between the past and the present, allowing us to connect with our ancestors and appreciate the rich cultural heritage they have left behind.

As we bid farewell to the mythical beings of the Americas, it is important to recognize their power in shaping our understanding of the world and our place within it. These creatures remind us of the boundless creativity and imagination within each of us and the enduring power of storytelling to bring people together and make sense of the unknown.

In conclusion, the fantastical creatures of the Americas have left an indelible mark on the cultural landscape of the continent and beyond. Their stories have been passed down through generations, evolving and adapting to the changing world. As we continue to explore the mysteries of our world and the depths of our imagination, there is no doubt that these mythical beings will continue to inspire and enchant us for generations to come.

6

OCEANIC AND AQUATIC MYTHICAL CREATURES

An image of alluring mermaids and mermen, half-human, half-fish beings.

The vast and mysterious depths of the world's oceans and waterways have long been a source of fascination and wonder for humankind. From the earliest seafaring civilizations to modern-day explorers, the allure of the unknown has captivated our imaginations and inspired countless myths, legends, and stories. Among the most enchanting of these tales are those that involve the myriad of mythical creatures said to inhabit the watery realms of our planet. These oceanic and aquatic beings, both benevolent and malevolent, have played a significant role in the folklore and mythology of cultures across the globe.

Oceanic and aquatic mythical creatures come in many shapes and sizes, ranging from the colossal and fearsome Kraken to the enchanting and alluring mermaids and mermen. These beings often embody the awe-inspiring power and beauty of the natural world, as well as the dangers and perils that lurk beneath the water's surface. They serve as a reminder of the vastness and mystery of the oceans and the potential for both wonder and terror within their depths.

In this chapter, we will journey through the enchanting world of oceanic and aquatic mythical creatures, exploring the legends and lore surrounding some of the most captivating beings ever to grace the pages of myth and folklore. We will delve into the stories mermaids and mermen, the alluring half-human, half-fish beings that have captured the hearts of sailors and land-dwellers alike. We will also investigate the mysteries of the Loch Ness Monster, Scotland's elusive water dweller, and the Leviathan, the ancient sea serpent of biblical lore.

Our voyage will take us to the far reaches of the world, from the mischievous water spirits of Japanese folklore, the Kappa, to the shape-shifting seal people of Celtic mythology, the Selkie. We will encounter the world serpent of Norse mythology, Jormungandr, and the deadly duo of Greek mythology, Charybdis and Scylla. Our exploration will also introduce us to the gigantic sea turtle of medieval legends, the Aspidochelone, and the fearsome creature of Australian Aboriginal mythology, the Bunyip.

As we navigate through these captivating tales, we will gain a deeper understanding of the enduring fascination with oceanic and aquatic mythical creatures and their important role in the cultural heritage of people worldwide. So, let us set sail on this exciting adventure and immerse ourselves in the enchanting world of oceanic and aquatic mythical creatures.

Please note that other creatures previously discussed that fall into this category include the Kraken (chapter 1), the Kappa (chapter 3), and the Selkie (chapter 2).

Mermaids and Mermen: The Alluring Half-Human, Half-Fish Beings

The enchanting world of oceanic and aquatic mythical creatures would be incomplete without mentioning mermaids and mermen, the alluring half-human, half-fish beings that have captivated the human imagination for centuries. These fascinating creatures have been a prominent part of folklore, literature, and art across various cultures, embodying the mysterious allure of the sea and the unknown depths beneath its surface.

Mermaids and mermen are typically depicted as having a human's upper body and a fish's lower body, complete with a long, scaly tail. In addition, their beauty and grace are often emphasized, with mermaids frequently portrayed as having long, flowing hair and enchanting voices that can lure sailors to their doom. Conversely, mermen are often depicted as strong and powerful, with impressive physiques and commanding presence.

The origin of mermaid and merman legends can be traced back to ancient civilizations, such as the Babylonians, Greeks, and Romans. For example, in Babylonian mythology, the god Oannes was said to be a fish-like being who emerged from the sea to teach humans wisdom and knowledge. Similarly, the Greek god Triton, the son of Poseidon, was depicted as a merman who wielded a powerful conch shell that could control the waves.

One of the most famous mermaid stories comes from Hans Christian Andersen's fairy tale, "The Little Mermaid." This poignant tale tells the story of a young mermaid who falls in love with a human prince and sacrifices her voice to gain legs and a chance to be with him. The story has been adapted into various forms, including the popular Disney animated film, which has further cemented the mermaid's place in popular culture.

Mermaids and mermen have also been associated with various superstitions and beliefs. In some cultures, they were believed to possess magical powers, such as the ability to control the weather or grant wishes. Sailors often viewed them as omens, with some believing that seeing a mermaid would bring bad luck or even cause a shipwreck. On the other hand, others believed that mermaids could be benevolent, guiding lost sailors to safety or even falling in love with them.

The fascination with mermaids and mermen has continued to thrive in recent years, with numerous books, movies, and television shows featuring these captivating creatures. The mermaid aesthetic has also become popular in fashion and design, with "mermaid hair" and mermaid-inspired clothing and accessories becoming trendy.

In conclusion, mermaids and mermen have long been a source of fascination and wonder, embodying the ocean's beauty, mystery, and danger. Their enduring appeal lies in their ability to capture our imagination and transport us to a magical world where the line between reality and fantasy is blurred. As we continue to explore the depths of our oceans and uncover new mysteries, the allure of these mythical beings will undoubtedly persist, enchanting generations to come.

The Loch Ness Monster: Scotland's Mysterious Water Dweller

Nestled within the picturesque Scottish Highlands lies the enigmatic Loch Ness, a deep and expansive freshwater lake that has captured the imagination of millions worldwide. The reason for this fascination is none other than the elusive Loch Ness Monster, affectionately known as "Nessie." This mysterious aquatic creature has been the subject of countless tales, sightings, and debates, making it one of the most famous mythical creatures ever.

The legend of the Loch Ness Monster dates back to ancient times, with the first recorded sighting occurring in the 6th century. Saint Columba, an Irish missionary, is said to have encountered a ferocious beast in the loch while attempting to save a man from drowning. Miraculously, the creature retreated upon hearing the saint's prayers, and the man was saved. Since then, numerous sightings and encounters have been reported, fueling the myth and intrigue surrounding Nessie.

Descriptions of the Loch Ness Monster vary, but most accounts depict it as a large, long-necked creature with humps on its back and a serpentine tail. Some believe that Nessie is a remnant of the prehistoric era, a surviving plesiosaur or another aquatic dinosaur that managed to escape extinction. Others propose that the creature is a giant eel or an unknown species yet to be discovered by science. Skeptics, on the other hand, argue that the sightings can be attributed to misidentifications of common animals, floating debris, or optical illusions caused by the loch's unique environmental conditions.

Despite the lack of concrete evidence, the Loch Ness Monster has become a cultural phenomenon and symbol of Scottish folklore. The creature has inspired numerous books, films, and television shows and a thriving tourism industry around Loch Ness. Visitors worldwide flock to the area, hoping to catch a glimpse of the legendary beast or to immerse themselves in the enchanting atmosphere of the loch and its surrounding landscape.

The enduring appeal of the Loch Ness Monster can be attributed to the human fascination with the unknown and the allure of ancient mysteries. As long as the depths of Loch Ness remain unexplored and the creature's existence unproven, the legend of Nessie will continue to captivate the hearts and minds of people everywhere. In a world where scientific advancements have demystified many of nature's wonders, the Loch Ness Monster serves as a reminder that there are still secrets waiting to be uncovered and that the world is a more magical place when shrouded in a bit of mystery.

The Leviathan: The Ancient Sea Serpent of Biblical Lore

The Leviathan, a colossal sea serpent of biblical lore, has captivated the imaginations of countless generations. This ancient creature, often described as a monstrous, twisting serpent or dragon, is said to dwell in the ocean's depths, ruling over the watery abyss with its fearsome presence. The Leviathan's origins can be traced back to the Old Testament, which is mentioned in several passages, most notably in the Book of Job and the Book of Isaiah. In these texts, the Leviathan is portrayed as a symbol of chaos and evil, a force to be reckoned with by mortals and gods alike.

The description of the Leviathan in the Book of Job is particularly vivid, painting a picture of a creature so immense and powerful that it defies human comprehension. The passage reads, "Its back has rows of shields tightly sealed together; each is so close to the next that no air can pass between. They are joined fast to one another; they cling together and cannot be parted." (Job 41:15-17, NIV) This description emphasizes the Leviathan's impenetrable armor and its seemingly invincible nature.

In addition to its physical prowess, the Leviathan is often associated with storms and natural disasters, further cementing its status as a symbol of chaos and destruction. In the Book of Isaiah, the Leviathan is described as a "gliding serpent" and a "coiling serpent" that will be slain by the Lord as part of a divine act of retribution (Isaiah 27:1, NIV). This passage suggests that the Leviathan's defeat will ultimately bring about a new era of peace and order, as the forces of chaos are defeated by divine intervention.

The Leviathan's influence extends beyond biblical texts, as it has also appeared in various mythologies and legends throughout history. In Jewish folklore, the Leviathan is sometimes depicted as a primordial sea monster that will be served as a feast for the righteous at the end of time. In medieval Christian art and literature, the Leviathan is often portrayed as a symbol of Satan or the embodiment of evil, further reinforcing its status as a force of chaos and destruction.

Despite its fearsome reputation, the Leviathan has also been the subject of fascination and admiration. Its immense size and power have inspired awe and wonder, and its mysterious nature has fueled countless tales of adventure and exploration. The Leviathan has even found its way into modern popular culture, appearing in various forms in literature, film, and video games.

In conclusion, the Leviathan is a prime example of the enduring fascination with oceanic and aquatic mythical creatures. This ancient sea serpent, with its immense power and chaotic nature, has captured the imaginations of countless generations, serving as a symbol of the untamed and mysterious depths of the ocean. As we continue to explore the world's oceans and uncover their secrets, the legend of the Leviathan remains a testament to the enduring allure of the unknown and the power of myth to inspire and captivate.

Jormungandr: The World Serpent of Norse Mythology

In the vast and mysterious realm of Norse mythology, one of the most awe-inspiring and fearsome creatures is Jormungandr, also known as the World Serpent or Midgard Serpent. This colossal sea serpent is said to encircle the entire world, holding its tail in its mouth, symbolizing the cyclical nature of life and the interconnectedness of all things. Jormungandr is a central figure in Norse mythology, and its presence has captivated the imagination of countless generations.

According to Norse legends, Jormungandr is one of the three monstrous offspring of the trickster god Loki and the giantess Angrboda. The gods, fearing the potential destruction these creatures could bring, cast Jormungandr into the ocean surrounding Midgard, the world of humans. There, the serpent grew so immense that it could encircle the entire world, its body forming a boundary between the land and the chaotic waters beyond.

Jormungandr's immense size and power are matched only by its enmity with the god Thor, the protector of humanity. The two are destined to face each other in a cataclysmic battle during Ragnarok, the end of the world in Norse mythology. In this apocalyptic event, Jormungandr will emerge from the ocean, causing massive floods and spewing venom into the air. Thor, wielding his mighty hammer Mjolnir, will confront the serpent in a battle that will shake the very foundations of the cosmos.

Despite their mutual animosity, Thor and Jormungandr have encountered each other several times before Ragnarok. One such encounter is the tale of Thor's fishing trip with the giant Hymir. In this story, Thor uses the head of an ox as bait and manages to hook Jormungandr on his fishing line. As the god struggles to pull the serpent from the depths, the two adversaries lock eyes, and the tension between them is palpable. However, at the last moment, Hymir, terrified by the sight of the World Serpent, cuts the fishing line, allowing Jormungandr to escape and return to its watery domain.

The legend of Jormungandr serves as a powerful metaphor for the forces of chaos and destruction that constantly threaten the world's stability. The serpent's presence in the ocean surrounding Midgard is a reminder of the precarious balance between order and chaos. The inevitable confrontation between Thor and Jormungandr during Ragnarok symbolizes the ultimate struggle between good and evil.

In conclusion, Jormungandr, the World Serpent of Norse mythology, is a fascinating and complex figure that embodies the eternal struggle between order and chaos. Its immense size, fearsome appearance, and destined clash with Thor have captured the imagination of countless generations, making it one of the most iconic and enduring symbols of Norse mythology. As we continue to explore the enchanting world of oceanic and aquatic mythical creatures, the legend of Jormungandr is a powerful reminder of the awe-inspiring and mysterious forces that lie beneath the surface of our world.

Charybdis and Scylla: The Deadly Duo of Greek Mythology

Few are as fearsome and intriguing as the deadly duo of Charybdis and Scylla in the vast and captivating world of oceanic and aquatic mythical creatures. These two monstrous beings have been immortalized in the annals of Greek mythology, striking terror into the hearts of sailors and adventurers who dared to venture into their treacherous domain. In this section, we will delve into the fascinating tales surrounding these two formidable creatures and explore the enduring allure of their legends.

Charybdis, often depicted as a massive whirlpool or a sea monster with a gaping maw, was said to reside in the Strait of Messina, the narrow water passage separating Sicily from the Italian mainland. According to myth, Charybdis was once a beautiful nymph and the daughter of Poseidon, the god of the sea, and Gaia, the goddess of the Earth. However, she incurred the wrath of Zeus, the king of the gods, when she flooded vast tracts of land and submerged entire cities. As punishment, Zeus transformed Charybdis into a monstrous whirlpool, forever doomed to swallow the sea and regurgitate it three times a day.

On the opposite side of the strait, lurking in a dark cave, lay Scylla, a terrifying creature with twelve feet, six long necks, and a grotesque head on each neck, each boasting a triple row of sharp teeth. Scylla was once a beautiful nymph as well, but she was transformed into a monster by the sorceress Circe out of jealousy. Scylla's insatiable hunger led her to devour any sailor who strayed too close to her lair, making the passage through the Strait of Messina, a perilous journey for even the most seasoned mariners.

The legends of Charybdis and Scylla have been immortalized in numerous ancient texts, most notably in Homer's epic poem, the Odyssey. In this tale, the hero Odysseus is forced to navigate the treacherous waters between the two monsters during his long and arduous journey home from the Trojan War. Faced with the impossible choice of losing his entire crew to Scylla or risking the destruction of his ship in the whirlpool of Charybdis, Odysseus chooses the lesser of two evils and sacrifices six of his men to Scylla's ravenous appetite.

The enduring fascination with Charybdis and Scylla can be attributed to their embodiment of the primal fears and dangers associated with the sea. These two mythical creatures represent nature's unpredictable and destructive forces that have challenged sailors and seafarers throughout history. Furthermore, the story of Odysseus' encounter with Charybdis and Scylla is a powerful allegory for the difficult choices and moral dilemmas that we all face in our lives.

In conclusion, the deadly duo of Charybdis and Scylla holds a unique and captivating place in the pantheon of oceanic and aquatic mythical creatures. Their legends continue to captivate and inspire, serving as a testament to the enduring allure of the enchanting world of Greek mythology and the timeless power of storytelling.

The Aspidochelone: The Gigantic Sea Turtle of Medieval Legends

The Aspidochelone, a colossal sea turtle of medieval legends, has captivated the imagination of many for centuries. This gargantuan creature, whose name is derived from the Greek words "aspis" (meaning shield) and "chelone" (meaning turtle), is said to be so enormous that it is often mistaken for an island. Unaware of the true nature of this deceptive beast, sailors would often anchor their ships to its massive shell, only to be dragged beneath the waves when the Aspidochelone decided to dive.

The origins of the Aspidochelone can be traced back to ancient Greek and Roman mythology, where it was known as the "Aspidochelon" or "Aspidoturtle." However, during the medieval period, the legend of this immense sea turtle flourished. The creature was often depicted in bestiaries, which were illustrated compendiums of real and mythical animals, and was used as a symbol of the devil and the dangers of the sea.

The Aspidochelone is not only known for its immense size but also for its cunning and evil nature. It is said to emit a sweet, alluring scent that attracts fish and other sea creatures to its back, providing a bountiful feast for the unsuspecting sailors who land upon it. Once the sailors had disembarked and set up camp, the Aspidochelone would suddenly submerge itself, drowning the unfortunate souls lured by its deception.

Despite its sinister reputation, the Aspidochelone is also associated with more benevolent qualities. In some versions of the legend, the creature is said to support the world on its back, much like the World Turtle of Hindu and Chinese mythology. In this interpretation, the Aspidochelone is seen as a symbol of stability and balance, holding the earth steady amidst the chaos of the ocean.

The legend of the Aspidochelone has endured throughout the centuries, inspiring countless works of art, literature, and even modern-day films. Its enduring appeal lies in the fascinating juxtaposition of its immense size and cunning nature, as well as the timeless allure of the unknown depths of the ocean. As long as humans continue to be drawn to the mysteries of the sea, the Aspidochelone will remain a captivating figure in the realm of oceanic and aquatic mythical creatures.

The Bunyip: The Fearsome Creature of Australian Aboriginal Mythology

The vast and diverse world of oceanic and aquatic mythical creatures would not be complete without delving into the rich and fascinating lore of Australian Aboriginal mythology. Among the many captivating tales passed down through generations, the story of the Bunyip stands out as one of the most fearsome and enigmatic creatures to inhabit the waters of the Australian continent.

The Bunyip, whose name is derived from the Wemba-Wemba or Wergaia language of the Aboriginal people of southeastern Australia, is a creature that has long been associated with swamps, billabongs, creeks, riverbeds, and waterholes. Descriptions of the Bunyip vary greatly, with some accounts depicting it as a large, hairy, dog-like creature with a long tail, while others describe it as having a crocodile-like head, a horse-like tail, and even the body of a giant starfish. Despite these varying descriptions, one thing remains consistent: the Bunyip is a creature to be feared and respected.

The Bunyip is said to be a highly territorial creature, fiercely guarding its watery domain against any who dare to intrude. It is believed that the eerie cries and growls that echo through the Australian wilderness at night are the warnings of the Bunyip, alerting those nearby to stay away from its territory. Those who ignore these warnings and venture too close to the Bunyip's lair risk being dragged beneath the water's surface, never to be seen again.

In addition to its fearsome reputation as a predator, the Bunyip also holds a significant place in Aboriginal cultural beliefs and practices. The creature is often regarded as a guardian of sacred water sources and is believed to possess supernatural powers. Some Aboriginal tribes even view the Bunyip as a punisher of wrongdoers sent by the spirits to maintain balance and order within their communities.

The Bunyip's presence in Australian Aboriginal mythology reminds us of the deep connection between the indigenous people and their natural environment. The creature's fearsome reputation and supernatural abilities reflect the respect and reverence with which the Aboriginal people view nature's powerful and often unpredictable forces.

In conclusion, the Bunyip is a captivating and enigmatic addition to the pantheon of oceanic and aquatic mythical creatures. Its fearsome reputation, diverse physical descriptions, and cultural significance within Australian Aboriginal mythology make it a fascinating subject for exploration and study. As we continue to delve into the world of mythical creatures, the Bunyip serves as a reminder of our enduring fascination with the unknown and the powerful role that mythology plays in shaping our understanding of the world around us.

The Enduring Fascination with Oceanic and Aquatic Mythical Creatures

Throughout history, the vast and mysterious depths of the oceans and other bodies of water have captured the imagination of countless cultures and civilizations. From the ancient Greeks and Norsemen to the indigenous peoples of Australia and Japan, the enchanting world of oceanic and aquatic mythical creatures has been a source of fascination, wonder, and even fear. These mythical beings, often embodying the power and unpredictability of the waters they inhabit, have become an integral part of our collective consciousness, transcending time and geographical boundaries.

The enduring appeal of these mythical creatures can be attributed to several factors. Firstly, the ocean is a realm of mystery and intrigue, with seemingly endless expanse and hidden depths. This vast, uncharted territory has long been a breeding ground for the human imagination, giving rise to countless legends and stories of fantastical beings that lurk beneath the waves. Furthermore, the ocean's inherent danger and unpredictability only heighten the allure of these mythical creatures, as they often embody the very forces of nature that humans have struggled to understand and control.

Secondly, oceanic and aquatic mythical creatures often possess a unique blend of human and animal characteristics, making them relatable and otherworldly. Mermaids and mermen, with their enchanting beauty and human-like emotions, have long been the subject of romantic tales and tragic love stories. At the same time, their fish-like tails and aquatic abilities remind us of their otherworldly origins, adding an element of mystery and intrigue to their allure.

Similarly, shape-shifting creatures like the Selkie and the Kappa blur the lines between humans and animals, challenging our understanding of the natural world and our place within it. These beings often serve as cautionary tales or moral lessons, reminding us of the consequences of our actions and the importance of respecting the delicate balance of nature.

Lastly, the enduring fascination with oceanic and aquatic mythical creatures can be attributed to their universal appeal. These stories and legends have been passed down through generations, transcending cultural and geographical boundaries. They serve as a testament to the power of storytelling, the human imagination, and our shared fascination with the unknown.

In conclusion, the enchanting world of oceanic and aquatic mythical creatures continues to captivate our imaginations, offering a glimpse into the depths of human creativity and our enduring fascination with the mysteries of the natural world. As we continue to explore and uncover the oceans' secrets, these mythical beings will remain a source of inspiration, wonder, and cautionary tales for generations to come.

7

HYBRID CREATURES: COMBINATIONS OF THE FAMILIAR AND THE STRANGE

An image of a powerful Minotaur standing guard in a labyrinth.

Throughout history, human beings have been captivated by the mysterious and the unknown. Our ancestors looked to the stars, the seas, and the depths of the earth to find explanations for the world around them. In their quest to make sense of the natural world, they created stories and legends passed down through generations. One of the most enduring and fascinating aspects of these tales is the presence of hybrid creatures - beings that combine the features of multiple animals or even humans and animals. These mythical beings have captured our imaginations for centuries and continue to do so today.

But what is it about hybrid creatures that makes them so alluring? One reason may be that they blend the familiar and the strange. Combining elements of animals we know and recognize with those that are more fantastical, these creatures become something entirely new and intriguing. They challenge our understanding of the natural world and force us to question the boundaries between reality and imagination.

Another reason for the appeal of hybrid creatures is their ability to embody complex and often contradictory qualities. They can be beautiful, terrifying, wise, foolish, or gentle and fierce. This duality makes them compelling characters in myths and legends, as they often serve as symbols of the human experience and the struggles we face in our own lives.

In this chapter, we will explore some of the most famous and captivating hybrid creatures from mythology. From the noble Centaur to the enigmatic sphinx, these beings have captured the hearts and minds of people for centuries. We will delve into their stories, symbolism, and why they continue to fascinate us today. So, let us embark on a journey into the world of hybrid creatures, where the familiar meets the strange, and the boundaries between reality and imagination blur.

Please note that other creatures previously discussed that fall into this category include the Griffin (chapter 1), the Minotaur (chapter 1), the Chimera (chapter 1), Mermaids and Mermen (chapter 6), the Naga (chapter 3), and the Sphinx (chapter 1).

The Centaur: Half-Human, Half-Horse Warriors

The Centaur, one of mythology's most iconic and captivating hybrid creatures, has long captured the imagination of storytellers and audiences alike. With a human's upper body and a horse's lower body, centaurs represent a fascinating blend of the familiar and the strange. These mythical beings embody the raw power and grace of the horse, combined with the intellect and emotions of a human, creating a complex and intriguing character that has endured through the ages.

Centaurs are believed to have originated in ancient Greek mythology, where they were often depicted as wild, untamed beings living in the remote and rugged landscapes of Thessaly and Arcadia. They were known for their prowess in battle, archery skill, and love for revelry and wine. In many myths, centaurs were portrayed as followers of the wine god Dionysus, indulging in drunken revelries that often led to violence and chaos.

Despite their wild and unruly nature, centaurs were not without their noble and wise representatives. The most famous is Chiron, a centaur renowned for his wisdom, knowledge, and skill in the healing arts. Chiron was a mentor and teacher to many great heroes of Greek mythology, including Achilles, Jason, and Heracles. Unlike his brethren, Chiron was depicted as a gentle and civilized being, embodying the more refined aspects of both human and horse.

The duality of the Centaur's nature – the struggle between their wild, animalistic instincts and their human intellect and emotions – has made them a popular subject in literature and art throughout history. From the epic battles of ancient Greek heroes to the allegorical tales of medieval writers, centaurs have explored themes of self-control, the balance between civilization and nature, and the inherent conflict within the human soul.

In modern times, centaurs continue to captivate our imagination, appearing in various forms of popular culture, such as fantasy novels, films, and role-playing games. They are often portrayed as noble and wise beings, living in harmony with nature and deeply understanding the world around them. This more positive portrayal of centaurs reflects our evolving understanding of the complex relationship between humans and the natural world and our ongoing fascination with combining the best qualities of both humans and animals.

In conclusion, as a hybrid creature, the Centaur represents a unique and enduring symbol of the struggle between our animal instincts and human intellect. Their dual nature allows us to explore the complexities of our existence, and their continued presence in our stories and myths is a testament to these fascinating beings' power and allure.

The Manticore: A Deadly Mix of Lion, Human, and Scorpion

The Manticore, a fearsome and deadly hybrid creature, has captivated the imagination of people for centuries. With the body of a lion, the face of a human, and the tail of a scorpion, the Manticore is a terrifying combination of some of the most powerful and dangerous creatures known to man. This mythical beast is believed to have originated in ancient Persia, where it was called "Mardkhora," meaning "man-eater." Over time, the Manticore's legend spread to other cultures, including ancient Greece and Rome, inspiring fear and awe.

The Manticore's most striking feature is its human-like face, often depicted with a sinister grin and sharp, menacing teeth. This unsettling visage is said to be capable of luring unsuspecting victims into a false sense of security before the creature strikes with its powerful lion's body and razor-sharp claws. However, the Manticore's face is a tool for deception and a weapon. It is said to be able to shoot poisonous spines at its prey, paralyzing them before moving in for the kill.

The Manticore's scorpion-like tail is another deadly weapon in its arsenal. This long, flexible appendage is tipped with a venomous stinger that can deliver a lethal dose of poison to any creature unfortunate enough to be struck by it. The Manticore's tail is also incredibly agile, allowing the beast to strike with lightning speed and deadly accuracy.

In addition to its fearsome physical attributes, the Manticore is often portrayed as an intelligent and cunning creature. For example, it is said to be capable of understanding human speech and even mimicking the voices of its victims to lure others into its deadly grasp. This combination of brute strength, venomous weaponry, and cunning intellect makes the Manticore a formidable foe in mythology.

Despite its fearsome reputation, the Manticore has also been associated with specific positive qualities. In some cultures, it is seen as a symbol of strength, courage, and power, and its image has been used to represent rulers and warriors. In other instances, the Manticore has been portrayed as a guardian figure, protecting sacred spaces and treasures from would-be thieves and invaders.

The Manticore's enduring appeal as a mythical creature lies in its unique combination of familiar and strange elements. By blending the characteristics of a lion, a human, and a scorpion, the Manticore represents a fascinating fusion of the natural and the supernatural, the known and the unknown. This deadly hybrid continues to captivate our imagination, reminding us of the power and mystery of the world's many mythological creatures.

The Harpy: Fierce and Terrifying Bird-Women

The harpy, a fearsome and captivating hybrid creature, has long been a source of fascination in mythology. These terrifying bird-women have captured the imagination of countless generations, embodying the perfect blend of beauty and horror. With a bird's body and a woman's head, harpies are often depicted as fierce, powerful, and merciless creatures. In this section, we will delve into the origins of the harpy, their role in various mythological tales, and the symbolism they represent.

The word "harpy" is derived from the Greek word "harpazein," which means "to snatch" or "to seize." This is a fitting name for these creatures, as they are often portrayed as agents of punishment, swooping down from the skies to abduct wrongdoers and carry them away. Harpies are believed to have originated in Greek mythology, but their influence has spread to various other cultures and mythologies over time.

One of the most famous tales involving harpies is the story of King Phineus, a blind prophet the gods punished for revealing their secrets. As a result, the gods sent harpies to torment him by stealing his food and befouling whatever they left behind. This continued until the Argonauts, a group of heroes led by Jason, arrived and drove the harpies away, freeing King Phineus from his torment.

Harpies have also been associated with "fury," a vengeful spirit that punishes those committing heinous crimes. In this context, the harpy symbolizes divine retribution, a reminder that the gods are always watching and that justice will be served.

Despite their fearsome reputation, harpies have also been depicted as beautiful and alluring creatures. This duality of beauty and terror is a common theme in mythology, as it reminds us that appearances can be deceiving and that even the most enchanting beings can harbor a dark side.

In art and literature, harpies have been portrayed in various ways, ranging from grotesque and monstrous to seductive and enchanting. This versatility has allowed the harpy to endure as a famous mythical creature, capturing the imagination of artists, writers, and readers alike.

In conclusion, the harpy is a captivating and terrifying hybrid creature that has captured the hearts and minds of those who encounter their stories. As agents of punishment and symbols of divine retribution, harpies serve as a reminder of the power and wrath of the gods. Their unique blend of beauty and horror has ensured their place in the pantheon of mythical creatures, and their legacy continues to inspire and captivate audiences.

The Satyr: Mischievous and Lustful Half-Human, Half-Goat Beings

The world of mythology is filled with fascinating and enigmatic creatures; among them, the Satyr holds a unique place. These half-human, half-goat beings have captivated the imagination of people for centuries, embodying nature's wild, untamed, and hedonistic aspects. This section will delve into the origins, characteristics, and stories surrounding these mischievous and lustful creatures.

Satyrs have their roots in ancient Greek mythology, where they were known as companions of Dionysus, the god of wine, fertility, and revelry. They were often depicted as having the upper body of a man and the lower body of a goat, complete with a tail and cloven hooves. Their faces were characterized by a prominent, upturned nose, pointed ears, and a beard, giving them a somewhat animalistic appearance. In Roman mythology, Satyrs were associated with the god Faunus, who was similar to the Greek god Pan and were called Fauns.

These hybrid creatures were known for their insatiable appetites for wine, music, and carnal pleasures. They were often portrayed as being in constant merriment and debauchery, playing flutes and dancing with nymphs in the forests and mountains. Their lustful nature was not limited to their pursuit of nymphs, as they were also known to chase after mortal women and even the occasional male traveler who crossed their path.

Despite their hedonistic tendencies, Satyrs were not considered evil beings. Instead, they were seen as embodiments of the untamed and chaotic aspects of nature, representing the wild and unpredictable forces that exist beyond the boundaries of human civilization. In this sense, they served as a reminder of the primal instincts and desires that lie within us, waiting to be unleashed.

There are several well-known stories involving Satyrs in Greek mythology. One such tale is that of the famous musician and poet Orpheus, who was said to have been taught the art of music by the Satyrs themselves. Another story tells of the encounter between the hero Theseus and a group of Satyrs who attempted to abduct his companion Helen. Theseus defeated the Satyrs and rescued Helen, earning their respect and admiration.

In conclusion, the Satyr is a fascinating example of a hybrid creature in mythology, combining the familiar aspects of human beings with the strange and wild characteristics of goats. Their mischievous and lustful nature has made them a popular subject in art and literature throughout history. They continue to symbolize the untamed forces that exist just beyond the edges of our civilized world. As we explore the many other hybrid creatures in mythology, we can appreciate the rich tapestry of stories and ideas woven to create these captivating beings.

The Enduring Fascination with Hybrid Creatures in Mythology

In conclusion, the enduring fascination with hybrid creatures in mythology can be attributed to the unique blend of the familiar and the strange that they represent. These mythical beings, which combine the characteristics of various animals and humans, have captivated the human imagination for centuries, transcending cultural and geographical boundaries. They serve as a testament to the creative power of the human mind and its ability to envision new possibilities by merging the known with the unknown.

Hybrid creatures often embody the qualities of the animals and humans they are composed of, resulting in a complex and intriguing mix of traits that can be both admirable and terrifying. They challenge our understanding of the natural world and force us to confront the limits of our imagination. Combining the strengths and weaknesses of different beings, these mythical hybrids symbolize the duality of human nature and the eternal struggle between good and evil.

Moreover, hybrid creatures often play significant roles in the myths and legends they inhabit, serving as powerful symbols of the human experience. They can represent our deepest fears, our greatest desires, or our most profound questions about the nature of existence. Through their stories, we can explore themes such as love, betrayal, courage, and wisdom, all while being transported to fantastical realms where the impossible becomes possible.

The continued fascination with hybrid creatures in mythology also speaks to our innate curiosity about the unknown and our desire to make sense of the world around us. These creatures challenge our preconceived notions of what is possible and force us to consider the boundaries between reality and fantasy. In doing so, they remind us of the power of storytelling and the importance of imagination in our lives.

As we continue to explore the rich tapestry of myths and legends worldwide, it is clear that hybrid creatures will remain an integral part of our collective imagination. They remind us of the boundless creativity of the human spirit and our ability to find meaning and inspiration in the most unexpected places. Whether fierce warriors, cunning tricksters, or enchanting sirens, these mythical beings continue to captivate and inspire us, leaving an indelible mark on our cultural heritage and understanding of the world.

8

DIVINE AND CELESTIAL BEINGS: MYTHICAL CREATURES OF THE HEAVENS

An image of mighty gods and goddesses ruling the heavens, filled with celestial grandeur.

Since the dawn of time, humanity has gazed up at the night sky, marveling at the vast expanse of twinkling stars and the mysterious celestial bodies that seem to dance across the heavens. Our ancestors, in their quest to understand the world around them, wove intricate tales and legends to explain the wonders of the cosmos. These stories gave birth to a pantheon of divine and celestial beings, mythical creatures embodying the universe's awe-inspiring power and beauty.

The celestial realm has long been a source of fascination and inspiration for countless cultures across the globe. From the ancient Greeks and Romans to the far reaches of Hindu and Buddhist mythology, the heavens have been populated with a diverse array of gods, goddesses, and mythical creatures that have captured the imagination of generations. These divine beings, often associated with the forces of nature, the elements, and the cosmos, have played a central role in the religious and spiritual beliefs of countless civilizations.

In this chapter, we will journey through the celestial realm, exploring the rich tapestry of mythical creatures that have graced the skies of our ancestors' imaginations. We will delve into the stories of the mighty gods and goddesses who rule over the heavens and the angels and archangels who serve as their messengers and protectors. In addition, we will encounter celestial dragons, guardians of the cosmic balance, and the legendary phoenix, a symbol of rebirth and immortality.

Our journey will take us to the mythical lands of ancient Greece, where we will meet the majestic Pegasus, the winged horse that has become synonymous with grace and beauty. We will venture into the realm of Norse mythology, where the valiant Valkyries guide fallen warriors to their eternal rest in the afterlife. We will explore the rich lore of Hindu and Buddhist mythology, encountering the powerful Garuda, the bird-like creature that serves as a mount for the gods, and the enchanting Apsaras and Gandharvas, celestial dancers and musicians who entertain the divine.

Finally, we will delve into the celestial bestiary of the Chinese constellations, discovering the mythical creatures associated with the stars for millennia. Throughout our journey, we will uncover the enduring legacy of these divine and celestial beings, examining their impact on art, literature, and the collective imagination of humanity.

So, let us spread our wings and take flight as we embark on this wondrous exploration of the mythical creatures that inhabit the celestial realm and discover the awe-inspiring stories that have captivated the hearts and minds of generations.

Please note that other creatures previously discussed that fall into this category include the Phoenix (chapter 1), the Pegasus (chapter 1), and the Garuda (chapter 3).

The Mighty Gods and Goddesses: Rulers of the Heavens

Throughout the ages, human civilizations have looked up to the heavens in awe and wonder, seeking answers to the mysteries of life and the cosmos. In their quest for understanding, they have created a pantheon of mighty gods and goddesses who rule over the celestial realm, wielding immense power and influence over the natural world and the lives of mortals. These divine beings, often depicted as larger-than-life figures with extraordinary abilities, have captured the imagination of countless generations and continue to inspire awe and reverence in the hearts of believers.

The gods and goddesses of the heavens are as diverse as the cultures that have given birth to them. In the ancient Greek pantheon, the supreme god Zeus ruled over the sky and the weather, wielding his mighty thunderbolts to maintain order and dispense justice. His wife, the goddess Hera, was the queen of the gods and the protector of marriage and childbirth. Together, they presided over a vast array of deities, each with their unique attributes and responsibilities.

In Norse mythology, the god Odin, the Allfather, ruled over the celestial realm of Asgard, where he presided over the Aesir, a tribe of powerful gods and goddesses. Odin was a god of wisdom, war, and poetry known for his relentless pursuit of knowledge. His wife, the goddess Frigg, was the patroness of marriage, motherhood, and domestic life and was revered for her prophetic powers.

The ancient Egyptians worshipped many gods and goddesses, each associated with specific aspects of the natural world and human life. Among the most prominent were the sun god Ra, who was believed to travel across the sky in a solar boat, bringing light and warmth to the world, and the goddess Isis, who was revered as the ideal mother and wife, and the protector of the dead.

In the Hindu pantheon, the god Vishnu is considered the preserver of the universe, responsible for maintaining cosmic order and balance. He is often depicted with four arms, symbolizing his omnipotence and omnipresence. His consort, the goddess Lakshmi, embodies wealth, fortune, and prosperity and is revered as the source of spiritual and material abundance.

These celestial rulers and countless other gods and goddesses from various mythologies have shaped human understanding of the divine and the cosmos for millennia. They have served as symbols of power, wisdom, love, and justice, guiding and inspiring those seeking their favor and protection. In their stories and legends, we find reflections of our hopes, fears, and aspirations, as well as a testament to the enduring human fascination with the mysteries of the heavens.

Angels and Archangels: Messengers and Protectors of the Divine

In the vast and awe-inspiring celestial realm, angels and archangels hold a special place as divine messengers and protectors. These ethereal beings, often depicted with wings and a halo, have captured the imagination of countless generations and continue to be a source of fascination and inspiration. This section will delve into the captivating world of angels and archangels, exploring their origins, roles, and significance in various mythologies and religious traditions.

Angels, derived from the Greek word "angelos," meaning "messenger," are supernatural beings that serve as intermediaries between the divine and human realms. They are found in various religious texts, including Christianity, Judaism, and Islam, as well as in the mythologies of ancient civilizations such as the Sumerians and Egyptians. Angels are typically portrayed as benevolent and compassionate beings tasked with guiding and protecting humans, delivering divine messages, and executing the will of the gods.

Archangels, on the other hand, are considered the highest-ranking angels, possessing greater power and authority than their angelic counterparts. They are often entrusted with the most important missions and responsibilities, such as leading the heavenly host in a battle against evil forces or overseeing the administration of divine justice. Some of the most well-known archangels include Michael, Gabriel, Raphael, and Uriel, each with their unique attributes and areas of expertise.

One of the most iconic and revered archangels is Michael, often depicted as a mighty warrior clad in armor and wielding a flaming sword. As the heavenly host's leader, Michael embodies courage, strength, and unwavering faith and is revered as the protector of the righteous and the vanquisher of evil. Michael plays a crucial role in the cosmic struggle between good and evil in Christian, Jewish, and Islamic traditions, defending the faithful against the forces of darkness and ensuring the triumph of divine justice.

Gabriel, another prominent archangel, is the divine messenger and the bringer of good news. In various religious texts, Gabriel is responsible for delivering important messages to key figures, such as the announcement of the birth of Jesus to the Virgin Mary in Christianity and the revelation of the Quran to the Prophet Muhammad in Islam. As the patron of communication and divine revelation, Gabriel is often associated with the virtues of wisdom, understanding, and clarity.

Raphael, the archangel of healing and guidance, is revered for his compassionate and nurturing nature. In various mythologies and religious traditions, Raphael is responsible for providing physical, emotional, and spiritual healing to those in need and guiding travelers and seekers on their journeys. His gentle and benevolent presence serves as a reminder of the divine love and care that permeates the universe.

Lastly, Uriel, the archangel of light and wisdom, is often depicted holding a flaming sword or a lantern, symbolizing his role as the illuminator of truth and the guardian of divine knowledge. Uriel is believed to provide guidance and insight to those who seek understanding, helping them navigate life's complexities and make wise decisions.

In conclusion, angels and archangels hold a unique and enduring place in the pantheon of mythical creatures, serving as divine messengers and protectors in various religious and cultural traditions. Their timeless appeal lies in their embodiment of humanity's highest virtues and aspirations, offering hope, inspiration, and solace in a world that is often fraught with uncertainty and strife. As we continue exploring the fascinating realm of divine and celestial beings, let us remember the profound wisdom and beauty these ethereal creatures represent and the enduring legacy they have left on our collective imagination.

The Celestial Dragons: Guardians of the Cosmic Balance

The celestial realm is home to many fascinating and awe-inspiring mythical creatures, each with unique roles and attributes. Among these divine beings, the Celestial Dragons stand out as powerful and enigmatic guardians of cosmic balance. These majestic creatures have been revered and admired across various cultures and mythologies, symbolizing wisdom, strength, and the eternal cycle of life.

In Chinese mythology, the Celestial Dragons are considered divine beings that control the forces of nature and maintain harmony in the universe. They are often depicted as long, serpentine creatures with four legs and adorned with intricate scales that shimmer like the stars in the night sky. The Chinese dragons are believed to have dominion over the elements, such as water, fire, earth, and air, and are associated with the changing seasons and celestial events.

The Azure Dragon, also known as the Dragon of the East, is one of the four celestial guardians in Chinese mythology. It represents the element of wood and is associated with the spring season. The Azure Dragon is said to bring prosperity and good fortune to those who honor it, and its presence is believed to ward off evil spirits and negative energies.

In Japanese mythology, the Celestial Dragons are known as Ryu or Tatsu, and they share many similarities with their Chinese counterparts. They are often depicted as powerful and wise beings who can control the weather and bless the people. The Japanese dragons are also associated with the Shinto religion, where they are considered divine messengers and protectors of sacred shrines.

In Western mythology, the Celestial Dragons are often portrayed as guardians of the heavens and the divine treasures. They are seen as symbols of power and authority, and their presence is believed to signify the divine will and cosmic order. The dragons in Western myths are usually depicted as fierce and formidable creatures with large wings and the ability to breathe fire.

The Celestial Dragons are revered for their immense power and wisdom and their role in maintaining the delicate balance of the cosmos. They are believed to be the guardians of the celestial gates, ensuring that the forces of good and evil remain in equilibrium. In this capacity, they serve as both protectors and enforcers of the divine order, ensuring the universe remains in harmony.

In conclusion, the Celestial Dragons are an integral part of the rich tapestry of mythical creatures that inhabit the celestial realm. Their presence in various mythologies highlights the universal fascination with these mysterious beings and their role in maintaining the cosmic balance. As guardians of the heavens and the divine order, the Celestial Dragons continue to captivate the imagination and inspire awe in those who seek to understand the mysteries of the universe.

The Valkyries: Choosers of the Slain and Guides to the Afterlife

The Valkyries hold a unique and awe-inspiring position in the vast tapestry of mythological beings. These powerful female figures, originating from Norse mythology, are known as the "Choosers of the Slain" and serve as guides to the afterlife for fallen warriors. The Valkyries are not only fierce and formidable, but they also embody the qualities of loyalty, honor, and duty.

The word "Valkyrie" is derived from Old Norse "valkyrja," which means "chooser of the slain." According to Norse mythology, the Valkyries are a group of divine beings who serve the chief god Odin. Their primary role is to select the bravest and most skilled warriors who have fallen in battle and guide them to the majestic halls of Valhalla, where they will join the ranks of the honored dead and prepare for the final battle of Ragnarok.

The Valkyries are often depicted as beautiful, strong, fearless women adorned in armor and riding magnificent winged horses. They are skilled in the arts of war and possess the power to influence the outcome of battles. In some accounts, they are described as shieldmaidens, while in others, they are portrayed as supernatural beings who can shape-shift and fly through the air.

The Valkyries play a crucial role in the Norse concept of the afterlife. Valhalla, the great hall of Odin, is reserved for the most valiant warriors who have proven their worth in battle. Here, the chosen warriors, known as the Einherjar, feast and train for the ultimate battle of Ragnarok, where they will fight alongside the gods against the forces of chaos and destruction. The Valkyries are responsible for selecting these warriors and ensuring their safe passage to Valhalla.

In addition to their duties as guides to the afterlife, the Valkyries also serve as Odin's messengers and emissaries. They are often sent to the mortal realm to deliver important messages or to carry out the gods' will. In some stories, they are even said to have the power to bestow blessings and gifts upon deserving mortals.

The legend of the Valkyries has endured throughout the centuries, capturing the imagination of countless generations. Their image has been immortalized in art, literature, and music, symbolizing strength, courage, and the eternal bond between the mortal and divine realms. The Valkyries remind us of the importance of honor and courage in the face of adversity, and their legacy continues to inspire awe and wonder in the hearts of those who encounter their mythic tales.

The Cherubim and Seraphim: The Highest Orders of Angelic Beings

In the vast and awe-inspiring celestial realm, the Cherubim and Seraphim hold a special place as the highest orders of angelic beings. These magnificent creatures are not only the closest to the divine presence but also play crucial roles in maintaining the harmony and balance of the heavens. This section will delve into the fascinating world of the Cherubim and Seraphim, exploring their origins, characteristics, and the vital functions they perform in the celestial hierarchy.

The Cherubim, often depicted as majestic beings with multiple wings and the faces of various creatures, are believed to be the guardians of the divine throne. Their origins can be traced back to ancient Mesopotamian mythology, where they were known as the "karibu," divine beings that protected sacred spaces. In the Hebrew Bible, the Cherubim are described as the powerful entities that guarded the entrance to the Garden of Eden after the expulsion of Adam and Eve. They are also mentioned in the construction of the Ark of the Covenant, where their images were placed on the mercy seat, symbolizing the presence of God.

The Seraphim, on the other hand, are often portrayed as radiant beings with six wings, two covering their faces, two covering their feet, and two with which they fly. The word "seraph" is derived from the Hebrew term "saraph," which means "to burn," signifying their intense and fiery nature. The Seraphim are primarily known for their role in the celestial choir, where they constantly praise the divine and maintain the harmony of the heavens. Their most famous appearance is in the biblical book of Isaiah, where the prophet has a vision of the Seraphim surrounding the throne of God, singing, "Holy, holy, holy is the Lord of hosts; the whole earth is full of his glory."

Both the Cherubim and Seraphim are endowed with immense wisdom, power, and beauty, reflecting the divine attributes they embody. They are often associated with the highest levels of spiritual attainment and are considered intermediaries between the divine and the lower orders of angels. Their presence in various religious texts and artistic representations serves as a reminder of the awe-inspiring majesty of the celestial realm and the profound connection between the divine and the created world.

In conclusion, the Cherubim and Seraphim stand as the epitome of the celestial hierarchy, embodying the divine attributes of wisdom, power, and beauty. Their roles as guardians of the divine throne and singers of the celestial choir highlight their importance in maintaining the harmony and balance of the heavens. As we continue to explore the rich tapestry of mythical creatures in the celestial realm, the enduring legacy of the Cherubim and Seraphim is a testament to the human fascination with the divine and the celestial, inspiring awe and wonder for generations to come.

The Celestial Beasts: Mythical Creatures of the Chinese Constellations

The celestial realm has always been a source of wonder and fascination for humankind. As we gaze upon the night sky, we cannot help but be captivated by the beauty and mystery of the stars and constellations. However, in Chinese mythology, the constellations are not merely a collection of stars but are also home to a group of extraordinary mythical creatures known as the Celestial Beasts. These awe-inspiring beings are deeply rooted in Chinese culture and have played a significant role in shaping the beliefs and traditions of the people.

The Celestial Beasts, also known as the Four Symbols, are four divine creatures representing the cardinal directions and the four seasons. Each beast is associated with a specific constellation, and together, they form an integral part of Chinese astrology and cosmology. So let us embark on a journey through the heavens and explore the fascinating world of these mythical creatures.

The Azure Dragon of the East, known as Qinglong in Chinese, is a majestic and powerful creature that symbolizes the element of wood and the season of spring. It is often depicted as a long, serpentine dragon with azure scales and a benevolent expression. The Azure Dragon is associated with the constellation of the eastern quadrant, which includes the seven mansions of the Chinese zodiac. As a symbol of power, wisdom, and prosperity, the Azure Dragon has been revered by emperors and commoners alike throughout Chinese history.

The Vermilion Bird of the South, or Zhuque, is a magnificent bird-like creature representing the element of fire and the summer season. With its vibrant red and orange plumage, the Vermilion Bird is a symbol of passion, transformation, and renewal. It is associated with the southern quadrant of the Chinese constellations, which includes the seven mansions of the zodiac. The Vermilion Bird is often depicted as a graceful phoenix, embodying the spirit of rebirth and the eternal cycle of life.

The White Tiger of the West, or Baihu, is a fierce and mighty feline creature that symbolizes the element of metal and the season of autumn. The White Tiger symbolizes courage, strength, and justice with its striking white fur and piercing blue eyes. It is associated with the western quadrant of the Chinese constellations, which includes the seven mansions of the zodiac. The White Tiger is often portrayed as a guardian and protector, ensuring the balance and harmony of the celestial realm.

The Black Tortoise of the North, known as Xuanwu in Chinese, is a unique and enigmatic creature representing the element of water and the winter season. It is often depicted as a hybrid being, combining the features of a tortoise and a snake. The Black Tortoise is associated with the northern quadrant of the Chinese constellations, including the zodiac's seven mansions. As a symbol of stability, endurance, and wisdom, the Black Tortoise has been revered as a guardian of the celestial realm and a source of divine guidance.

In conclusion, the Celestial Beasts of the Chinese constellations are a testament to the rich and diverse tapestry of Chinese mythology. These divine creatures embody the natural elements and seasons and serve as powerful symbols of the human virtues and values that have shaped Chinese culture for millennia. As we continue to explore the heavens and unravel the mysteries of the universe, the enduring legacy of the Celestial Beasts serves as a reminder of the timeless wisdom and beauty of ancient mythology.

The Apsaras and Gandharvas: Celestial Dancers and Musicians of Hindu Mythology

In Hindu mythology's vast and enchanting world, the celestial realm is home to a myriad of divine and mystical beings. Among these heavenly inhabitants are the Apsaras and Gandharvas, ethereal creatures known for their unparalleled beauty, grace, and talent in dance and music. These celestial artists play a significant role in Hindu mythology, serving as symbols of joy, inspiration, and the transcendent power of art.

The Apsaras, often called the "nymphs of the heavens," are a group of celestial dancers and enchantresses who reside in the court of Lord Indra, the king of the gods. These divine beings are renowned for their breathtaking beauty and ability to captivate the hearts of gods and mortals with their mesmerizing dance performances. In addition to their artistic prowess, the Apsaras are also known for their role in various mythological tales, where they often serve as agents of divine intervention or as the embodiment of the rewards and temptations that await those who tread the path of righteousness or vice.

On the other hand, the Gandharvas are celestial musicians often depicted as half-human and half-bird creatures. They are said to possess unparalleled musical skill, with their heavenly melodies capable of soothing the souls of gods and mortals alike. The Gandharvas are also known for their role as the guardians of the Soma, the sacred elixir of immortality, which they protect from the demons who seek to steal it for their nefarious purposes. In addition to their musical talents, the Gandharvas are also skilled warriors, often accompanying the gods into battle and using their divine melodies to inspire and invigorate their allies.

The Apsaras and Gandharvas are often depicted together in Hindu art and literature, symbolizing the harmonious union of dance and music. Their celestial performances are so captivating that they can transport their audience to a state of divine ecstasy, allowing them to momentarily transcend the mundane concerns of the mortal world and experience a glimpse of the sublime beauty and bliss of the heavenly realm.

The enduring appeal of the Apsaras and Gandharvas in Hindu mythology can be attributed to their embodiment of the transcendent power of art and the human desire for beauty, inspiration, and spiritual elevation. Through their divine dance and music, these celestial beings remind us of the transformative potential of art and its ability to uplift our spirits, nourish our souls, and connect us with the divine. In a world that is often beset by strife and suffering, the Apsaras and Gandharvas serve as a beacon of hope and a testament to the enduring power of beauty, grace, and creativity to illuminate the darkest corners of the human experience and guide us toward a higher plane of existence.

The Enduring Legacy of Divine and Celestial Beings in Mythology

Throughout the ages, divine and celestial beings have captivated the imagination, inspiring awe, wonder, and reverence. Moreover, these mythical creatures of the heavens have played a significant role in shaping the beliefs, values, and cultural identity of various civilizations across the globe. As we conclude our exploration of these fascinating beings, it is essential to reflect on their enduring legacy and the profound impact they continue to have on our collective consciousness.

The tales of gods and goddesses, angels and archangels, celestial dragons, and other heavenly beings have been passed down through generations, transcending time and geographical boundaries. These stories have entertained and enthralled us and provided us with valuable insights into the human condition, our relationship with the cosmos, and the eternal quest for meaning and purpose.

The rich tapestry of divine and celestial beings in mythology serves as a testament to the creative genius of our ancestors, who sought to make sense of the world around them and the mysteries of the universe. Moreover, these mythical creatures embody humanity's hopes, fears, aspirations, and ideals, reflecting our innate desire to connect with something greater than ourselves.

In contemporary times, the influence of these celestial beings can still be felt in various aspects of our lives, from art and literature to religion and spirituality. The enduring appeal of these mythical creatures lies in their ability to resonate with our deepest emotions and experiences, offering solace, guidance, and inspiration in times of need.

Moreover, the study of divine and celestial beings in mythology can also be a powerful tool for fostering intercultural understanding and appreciation. By exploring the similarities and differences between the celestial beings of various mythological traditions, we can better appreciate the shared human experience and the universal themes that unite us all.

In conclusion, mythology's legacy of divine and celestial beings is rich and multifaceted, reflecting the complexity and diversity of human thought and imagination. As we continue to delve into the realm of the heavens and uncover the secrets of these mythical creatures, we are reminded of our potential for creativity, resilience, and transcendence. May the stories of these celestial beings continue to inspire and guide us on our journey through life as we strive to reach for the stars and unlock the mysteries of the universe.

9

DARK AND MALEVOLENT ENTITIES: CREATURES OF THE UNDERWORLD

An image depicting the demonic hierarchy, showcasing the rulers of the underworld.

Throughout the ages, humankind has been captivated by the mysteries of the unknown, the unexplained, and the supernatural. From the earliest cave paintings to the most advanced virtual reality experiences, we have sought to explore and understand the darker aspects of our world and the creatures that inhabit it. In this chapter, we will delve into the shadows of mythology and uncover the dark and malevolent entities that have haunted our collective imagination for centuries.

These creatures of the underworld have taken many forms, from the bloodthirsty vampires of Eastern Europe to the shape-shifting werewolves of ancient Rome. They have been the subjects of countless stories, legends, and folklore, each more terrifying than the last. Yet, despite their fearsome reputations, these mythical beings continue to fascinate and enthrall us, reminding us of the darker side of human nature and the primal fears that still lurk within our subconscious minds.

As we journey through the realms of darkness, we will encounter a diverse array of sinister beings, each with unique characteristics and abilities. We will explore the demonic hierarchy that governs the underworld and the various types of undead creatures that roam the earth in search of human prey. We will also venture into the heart of the forest to confront the insatiable hunger of the Wendigo.

In addition to examining the origins and characteristics of these dark mythical creatures, we will also consider the cultural and psychological factors that have contributed to their enduring popularity. From ancient myths and legends to modern horror films and literature, these malevolent entities have served as a means of exploring our deepest fears and anxieties and understanding the darker aspects of the human psyche.

So, prepare yourself for a thrilling and chilling journey into the shadows of mythology as we uncover the dark and evil entities that have haunted our dreams and nightmares for millennia. But be warned: once you have entered the realm of the underworld, there is no turning back.

Please note that other creatures previously discussed that fall into this category include the Kraken (chapter 1), the Wendigo (chapter 5), and the Gorgons (chapter 2).

The Demonic Hierarchy: Rulers of the Underworld

As we delve deeper into the shadows of mythology, we encounter a realm that has long captivated the human imagination: the underworld. This dark and mysterious place is home to many malevolent entities, each with unique powers and abilities. Among these sinister beings is a hierarchy, a structured order that governs the demonic realm. In this section, we will explore the demonic hierarchy and the rulers of the underworld, shedding light on the forces that govern this enigmatic realm.

The concept of a demonic hierarchy can be traced back to ancient cultures and religious traditions. In Christianity, for example, the hierarchy of demons is often depicted as a reflection of the angelic hierarchy, with Satan, the fallen angel, reigning supreme as the ruler of the underworld. Similarly, in Hinduism, the demon king Ravana is said to rule over a vast army of demonic beings. While the specifics of the demonic hierarchy may vary across different cultures and belief systems, the underlying theme remains the same: a structured order of malevolent entities, each with their unique powers and abilities.

At the top of the demonic hierarchy, we find the rulers of the underworld. These powerful beings are often depicted as the embodiment of evil, commanding legions of lesser demons and exerting their influence over the mortal world. Some of the most well-known rulers of the underworld include Satan in Christianity, Hades in Greek mythology, and Anubis in Egyptian mythology. These rulers are often associated with death, destruction, and chaos, and their presence is a constant reminder of the dark forces that lurk just beyond the veil of our reality.

Beneath the rulers of the underworld, we find a diverse array of demonic beings, each with unique powers and abilities. These demons often serve as the enforcers of the underworld, carrying out the will of their dark masters. Among these demonic entities, we find creatures such as the succubi and incubi, seductive demons that prey on the desires of mortals; the imps, mischievous tricksters that delight in causing chaos and mischief; and the hellhounds, ferocious beasts that guard the gates of the underworld.

As we descend further into the demonic hierarchy, we encounter the lesser demons, beings that, while not as powerful as their higher-ranking counterparts, still possess the ability to wreak havoc on the mortal world. These lesser demons often serve as foot soldiers in the armies of the underworld, carrying out the orders of their demonic masters. Some examples of lesser demons include the malebranche, a group of demons that torment the souls of the damned in Dante's Inferno, and the jinn, supernatural creatures in Islamic mythology that can be either benevolent or malevolent.

In conclusion, the demonic hierarchy is a fascinating and complex aspect of the mythology surrounding the underworld. By exploring the various ranks and roles of these dark and malevolent entities, we gain a deeper understanding of the forces that govern this enigmatic realm. From the underworld rulers to the lesser demons serving them, the demonic hierarchy is a testament to the enduring allure of dark mythical creatures and the captivating power of the human imagination.

Vampires: The Undead Predators of the Night

Vampires, the enigmatic and fearsome creatures of the night, have haunted the pages of literature and cinema screens for centuries. These undead predators, with their insatiable thirst for human blood, have become a staple in dark mythology. But where did these sinister beings originate, and what about them continues to captivate and terrify us?

The concept of the vampire can be traced back to ancient civilizations, where tales of blood-sucking demons and spirits were prevalent. In Mesopotamian mythology, the goddess Lamashtu was known to prey on the blood of infants, while the Greeks spoke of the vrykolakas, a revenant that fed on the living. However, the vampire as we know it today began to take shape during the Middle Ages in Eastern Europe.

The word "vampire" is derived from the Slavic term "upir," which describes a blood-drinking revenant.

The vampire's appearance has evolved, but specific characteristics have remained consistent. These nocturnal creatures are often depicted as pale-skinned, with elongated fangs and an aversion to sunlight. In addition, they are said to possess supernatural strength, speed, and the ability to transform into animals such as bats or wolves. Some legends also attribute the power of hypnotism and mind control to these malevolent beings.

One of the most iconic aspects of vampire lore is their need to feed on human blood. This insatiable hunger is a means of sustenance and a way to maintain their immortality. Feeding is often portrayed as both sensual and violent, a dance between predator and prey that ends in the victim's life force being drained away. This duality of seduction and horror is a critical element of the vampire's enduring appeal.

Vampires are also known for their vulnerability to specific objects and rituals. The most well-known of these is the stake through the heart, which is the only way to kill a vampire. Other methods of warding off these creatures include garlic, holy water, and crucifixes. These weaknesses humanize the vampire, making them more relatable and, in turn, more frightening.

Over the years, the vampire has been portrayed in various forms, from the monstrous and grotesque to the suave and sophisticated. The latter image was popularized by Irish author Bram Stoker in his 1897 novel, "Dracula," which introduced the world to the charismatic and enigmatic Count Dracula. This portrayal of the vampire as a charming and cultured aristocrat has since become a staple in popular culture, with countless adaptations and reinterpretations gracing page and screen.

In conclusion, vampires have remained prominent in dark mythology due to their unique blend of seduction and terror. These undead predators of the night embody our deepest fears and desires, serving as a cautionary tale of the consequences of succumbing to our baser instincts. As long as humans are fascinated by the darkness within ourselves, the vampire will continue to haunt our collective imagination.

Werewolves: Shape-shifting Beasts of Legend

In the realm of dark and malevolent entities, werewolves hold a special place in the pantheon of mythical creatures. These shape-shifting beasts of legend have haunted the human imagination for centuries, striking fear into the hearts of those who dare to venture into the moonlit night. Werewolves, also known as lycanthropes, are humans who possess the ability to transform into wolves or wolf-like creatures, often under the influence of a full moon. This metamorphosis is typically accompanied by an insatiable bloodlust and a primal urge to hunt, making werewolves a terrifying force to be reckoned with.

The origins of werewolf mythology can be traced back to ancient civilizations, where stories of humans transforming into animals were a common theme in folklore. In Greek mythology, the tale of Lycaon, a king transformed into a wolf by Zeus as punishment for his wicked deeds, is an early example of the werewolf myth. Similarly, in Norse mythology, the Saga of the Volsungs tells the story of a father and son who don wolf pelts and gain the power to transform into wolves for some time.

Throughout history, werewolf legends have evolved and adapted to the cultural context in which they were told. For example, in medieval Europe, werewolves were often associated with witchcraft and devil worship, and those accused of lycanthropy were subjected to the same brutal persecution as suspected witches. In more recent times, the werewolf has become a staple of Gothic literature and horror films, with iconic portrayals such as Lon Chaney Jr.'s performance in the 1941 film "The Wolf Man" and the chilling transformation scene in the 1981 movie "An American Werewolf in London."

The mythology surrounding werewolves is rich and varied, with different cultures offering unique explanations for the origins of the curse and the methods by which it can be transmitted or cured. Some legends suggest that lycanthropy is a hereditary condition passed down through generations of afflicted families. Others propose that the curse can be acquired through a bite or scratch from an existing werewolf or by making a pact with the devil. In some traditions, the transformation can be controlled or reversed through magical talismans, potions, or rituals.

Despite the diverse array of werewolf myths, certain themes and motifs remain consistent across cultures. The full moon is often associated with the werewolf transformation, symbolizing the primal, untamed nature of the beast within. The struggle between the human and animal aspects of the werewolf's dual nature is a recurring theme, reflecting the broader human struggle to balance our rational, civilized selves with our more primitive, instinctual desires.

In conclusion, werewolves represent a fascinating and enduring aspect of dark mythical creatures. Their shape-shifting abilities and primal instincts tap into our deepest fears and remind us of the wild, untamed forces that lurk beneath the surface of our humanity. As we continue exploring the shadowy realms of mythology, the werewolf will remain a captivating and terrifying figure in our collective imagination.

Ghouls and Revenants: The Restless Dead

As we delve deeper into the shadows of mythology, we encounter two of the most chilling and macabre creatures that have haunted the human psyche for centuries: ghouls and revenants. These restless dead beings have been the subject of countless tales, legends, and nightmares, striking fear into the hearts of those who dare to cross their paths. This section will explore the origins, characteristics, and cultural significance of these dark and malevolent entities.

Ghouls, originating from Arabian folklore, are ghastly creatures that lurk in desolate places such as graveyards, ruins, and deserts. They feast on the flesh of the dead and, in some tales, even prey on the living. Ghouls are often depicted as shape-shifting beings, able to assume the form of animals or even the deceased person they have consumed. This ability to transform allows them to deceive and lure unsuspecting victims to their doom. The concept of the ghoul has evolved, with modern interpretations often portraying them as undead, zombie-like creatures.

Revenants, on the other hand, have their roots in European folklore and are believed to be the reanimated corpses of the deceased. Unlike ghouls, revenants are not driven by a hunger for flesh but rather by a desire for vengeance or to fulfill an uncompleted task. They are often depicted as retaining their human appearance, albeit decayed and grotesque. Revenants are known to possess supernatural strength and are impervious to conventional weapons, making them formidable adversaries.

The fear and fascination surrounding ghouls and revenants can be attributed to the universal human fear of death and the unknown. These creatures embody the idea that death may not be the end but a gateway to a darker, more terrifying existence. They also serve as a reminder of the consequences of one's actions in life, as revenants are often portrayed as seeking retribution for past wrongs.

Throughout history, ghouls and revenants have been the subject of numerous literary works, films, and other forms of popular culture. From the classic Gothic novels of the 19th century to modern horror films and video games, these creatures continue to captivate and terrify audiences worldwide. Their enduring appeal lies in their ability to tap into our deepest fears and force us to confront the darker aspects of our nature.

In conclusion, ghouls and revenants are two of the most chilling and macabre creatures in the realm of dark mythical entities. Their origins in Arabian and European folklore, terrifying characteristics, and cultural significance make them fascinating subjects for exploration and storytelling. As we continue our journey through the underworld of mythology, we are reminded of the power of these dark and malevolent beings to both frighten and intrigue us and of the enduring allure of the restless dead.

The Nuckelavee: A Horrifying Hybrid of Man and Beast

The Nuckelavee is a terrifying creature that has haunted the folklore of the Orkney Islands, an archipelago in the Northern Isles of Scotland. This monstrous hybrid of man and beast is said to emerge from the sea, bringing death and destruction to those unfortunate enough to cross its path. The Nuckelavee is a prime example of the dark and malevolent entities that lurk within mythology, embodying the fears and anxieties of the people who once believed in its existence.

The Nuckelavee's appearance is a grotesque amalgamation of human and equine features. Its body is that of a large, skinless horse, with its exposed muscles and sinews giving it a horrifying, raw appearance. In addition, the creature's head is disproportionately large, with a single, bloodshot eye that is said to burn with a malevolent red glow. However, the most disturbing aspect of the Nuckelavee is the human torso that sprouts from its back, complete with a head and arms that can stretch out to grab its victims.

The Nuckelavee is not only terrifying in appearance but also in its actions. It is said to have an insatiable appetite for destruction, causing droughts, crop failures, and the spread of disease among livestock. The creature is also known to have a particular hatred for humans, and its breath is said to be so toxic that it can wilt crops and sicken those who inhale it. The Nuckelavee's malevolence is further demonstrated by its habit of pursuing and tormenting its victims, often driving them to madness or death.

Despite its fearsome reputation, the Nuckelavee has its weaknesses. The creature is said to be unable to cross fresh water, making rivers and streams a haven for those fleeing its wrath. Additionally, the Nuckelavee is said to be repelled by the burning of seaweed. This practice was once common in the Orkney Islands to produce a type of ash used in agriculture. This aversion to seaweed smoke has led some to speculate that the Nuckelavee may have been a symbolic representation of the harmful effects of this practice on the environment and the islanders' health.

The Nuckelavee is a chilling reminder of the dark and evil forces within the realm of mythology. This horrifying hybrid of man and beast embodies the fears of the unknown and the destructive power of nature, serving as a cautionary tale for those who would underestimate the power of the world's darker forces. As we continue to explore the shadowy corners of myth and legend, the Nuckelavee stands as a testament to the enduring allure of these dark and mysterious creatures.

The Dybbuk: Possessing Spirits of the Damned

The Dybbuk, a malevolent spirit from Jewish folklore, has long been a source of fascination and terror. These restless souls, unable to find peace in the afterlife, seek refuge in the bodies of the living, possessing them and causing untold suffering and chaos. The word "dybbuk" itself is derived from the Hebrew term "dibbuk," which means "to cling" or "to adhere," reflecting the spirit's tenacious grip on its host.

The origin of the Dybbuk can be traced back to the Kabbalistic texts of the 16th century, where it was believed that the souls of the wicked were condemned to wander the earth, unable to find rest. These tormented spirits, filled with anger and despair, would seek out vulnerable individuals to possess, often targeting those who were emotionally or spiritually weak.

Once a Dybbuk has taken possession of a person, it is said to cause a wide range of physical and psychological symptoms, including sudden mood swings, unexplained illnesses, and even violent outbursts. The possessed individual may also exhibit knowledge of events or languages they have no prior experience with, as the Dybbuk shares its memories and experiences with its host.

Exorcising a Dybbuk is no easy task and often requires the intervention of a skilled rabbi or spiritual leader. The exorcism ritual, known as a "dybbuk exorcism," typically involves reciting prayers and incantations and using sacred objects such as a Torah scroll or a shofar (a ram's horn). The goal of the exorcism is to compel the Dybbuk to leave its host and return to the afterlife, where it can finally find peace.

The Dybbuk has been the subject of numerous books, plays, and films, most notably the 1914 Yiddish play "The Dybbuk" by S. Ansky, which was later adapted into a film in 1937. The concept of a possessing spirit has also been explored in other cultures and mythologies, such as the jinn in Islamic folklore and the malevolent spirits of the Native American tradition.

The enduring allure of the Dybbuk lies in its ability to tap into our deepest fears and insecurities. The idea of losing control of our bodies and minds to an unseen force is a terrifying prospect, and the Dybbuk serves as a potent reminder of the darker side of the human psyche. As we delve into the shadows of mythology, the Dybbuk stands as a chilling example of the power of the supernatural to both fascinate and terrify us.

The Strigoi: The Soul-Stealing Wraiths of Eastern Europe

The Strigoi, originating from the rich folklore of Eastern Europe, are terrifying creatures that have haunted the imaginations of countless generations. These malevolent beings are known for their insatiable hunger for human souls, striking fear into the hearts of those who dare to speak their name. In this section, we will delve into the dark world of the Strigoi, exploring their origins, characteristics, and the chilling tales surrounding them.

The word "Strigoi" is derived from the ancient Roman term "Strix," which referred to a nocturnal bird of ill omen that fed on human flesh and blood. Over time, the concept of the Strix evolved into the Strigoi, a supernatural creature that shares many similarities with the modern-day vampire. The Strigoi are predominantly associated with Romanian folklore, but their influence can also be found in the myths and legends of other Eastern European cultures.

The Strigoi are believed to be the restless souls of the deceased who have returned from the grave to torment the living. They are often depicted as pale, gaunt figures with sharp fangs and long, claw-like nails. The Strigoi possesses many supernatural abilities, including shape-shifting, invisibility, and the power to control animals such as wolves and bats. However, their most fearsome ability is their penchant for stealing the souls of their victims, leaving behind lifeless husks devoid of any essence.

There are several ways in which a person can become a Strigoi. Some are born with the curse, destined to transform into these soul-stealing wraiths upon death. Others may be turned into Strigoi due to a curse or through the intervention of dark magic. Finally, in some cases, individuals who have led, particularly wicked lives may return as Strigoi to continue their reign of terror in the afterlife.

The legends surrounding the Strigoi are tales of brave heroes and cunning villagers who have outwitted or defeated these fearsome creatures. One common method of dealing with a Strigoi is to drive a stake through its heart, pinning it to the ground and preventing it from rising again. Other methods include decapitation, burning the body, or burying the corpse with a sickle around its neck to sever the head should the Strigoi attempt to rise.

Despite the gruesome nature of these tales, the Strigoi continues to captivate the minds of those who encounter their stories. They serve as a chilling reminder of the darker aspects of human nature and the enduring power of myth and legend. As we explore the shadowy corners of the world's folklore, the Strigoi stand as a testament to the timeless allure of the macabre and the unknown.

The Enduring Allure of Dark Mythical Creatures

Throughout history, the human imagination has been captivated by the dark and mysterious realm of mythical creatures. From the depths of the underworld to the shadows of the forest, these evil entities have haunted our dreams and inspired countless tales of terror and fascination. As we have explored in this chapter, the allure of dark mythical creatures is deeply rooted in our collective psyche, reflecting our deepest fears, desires, and curiosities.

One of the primary reasons for the enduring appeal of these creatures is their ability to embody the darker aspects of human nature. In many ways, they serve as a mirror, reflecting our capacity for evil and the potential consequences of our actions. By personifying these darker impulses, mythical creatures allow us to confront and explore our inner demons in a safe and imaginative context.

Moreover, dark mythical creatures often serve as cautionary tales, warning us of the dangers lurking in our world's shadows. From the insatiable hunger of the Wendigo to the soul-stealing Strigoi, these creatures remind us of the perils of succumbing to our baser instincts and the importance of maintaining a balance between good and evil. In this way, they provide valuable moral lessons that continue to resonate with audiences across generations and cultures.

Additionally, the enduring allure of dark mythical creatures can be attributed to their ability to tap into our innate fascination with the unknown. Humans are naturally drawn to the mysteries of the world around us. The realm of mythical creatures offers a rich and diverse landscape for our imaginations to explore; whether it's the terrifying depths of the ocean inhabited by the Kraken or the hidden corners of the forest where the Nuckelavee dwells, these creatures invite us to venture beyond the boundaries of our everyday reality and delve into the uncharted territories of the supernatural.

Furthermore, the captivating nature of dark mythical creatures is enhanced by their versatility as storytelling devices. Throughout history, these entities have been used to explore a wide range of themes and emotions, from the tragic love story of the vampire to the psychological horror of the werewolf. This adaptability allows dark mythical creatures to remain relevant and engaging, as they can be continually reimagined and reinvented to suit the needs of contemporary audiences.

In conclusion, the enduring allure of dark mythical creatures lies in their ability to reflect our deepest fears and desires, serve as cautionary tales, ignite our fascination with the unknown, and adapt to the ever-changing landscape of human storytelling. As long as we continue to grapple with the complexities of our nature and seek to understand the mysteries of the world around us, these dark and malevolent entities will continue to captivate our imaginations and haunt our dreams.

10

THE ROLE OF MYTHICAL CREATURES IN MODERN CULTURE AND MEDIA

An image of various mythical creatures interacting in a modern cityscape.

Since the dawn of human civilization, mythical creatures have captivated the imagination of people across cultures and continents. These fantastical beings, often possessing extraordinary powers and abilities, have been woven into the fabric of our collective consciousness, serving as symbols of our deepest fears, desires, and aspirations. From the mighty dragons of ancient China to the elusive unicorns of medieval Europe, mythical creatures have transcended time and space, continuing to enchant and inspire us in the modern era.

But what is it about these mythical beings that have allowed them to endure and thrive in contemporary culture and media? The answer lies in their inherent ability to tap into the human psyche, reflecting our innate fascination with the unknown and the supernatural. As we navigate the complexities of the modern world, mythical creatures offer us an escape from the mundane, a window into a realm of wonder and possibility where the ordinary rules of reality no longer apply.

In this chapter, we will explore how mythical creatures have permeated modern culture and media, from literature and cinema to television, gaming, and beyond. We will examine the enduring appeal of these fantastical beings, delving into their symbolic significance and their psychological impact on society. Furthermore, we will discuss the role of mythical creatures in shaping our cultural identity and heritage, as well as their influence on art, design, fashion, and advertising.

As we embark on this journey through the world of mythical creatures in modern culture and media, we will discover that their allure is far from a mere relic of the past. Instead, these enigmatic beings continue to evolve and adapt, finding new ways to captivate and enthrall us in an ever-changing landscape of technology and storytelling. In doing so, they remind us of the power of imagination and the enduring human need for wonder, mystery, and magic.

Mythical Creatures in Literature: From Ancient Epics to Modern Bestsellers

Mythical creatures have been an integral part of human storytelling since the dawn of civilization. From ancient epics to modern best-sellers, these fantastical beings have captured the imagination of readers and writers alike, serving as powerful symbols and allegories that reflect our deepest fears, desires, and aspirations. In this section, we will explore the enduring presence of mythical creatures in literature, tracing their evolution from the earliest myths and legends to the contemporary works that continue to enchant and inspire us today.

The origins of mythical creatures in literature can be traced back to the ancient world, where they played a central role in the mythologies and religious beliefs of various cultures. In the Mesopotamian Epic of Gilgamesh, for example, the hero encounters the fearsome Humbaba, a monstrous giant with the face of a lion and the body of a scaly dragon. Similarly, the Greek poet Homer's Iliad and Odyssey are filled with a pantheon of gods, monsters, and supernatural beings, such as the Cyclops, the Sirens, and the shape-shifting Proteus.

As literature evolved over the centuries, so too did the portrayal of mythical creatures. In the Middle Ages, the chivalric romances of King Arthur and his knights introduced a new generation of mythical beings, including the enigmatic Lady of the Lake, the mischievous Puck, and the fearsome Questing Beast. These stories entertained their audiences and served as moral allegories, teaching important lessons about courage, honor, and the nature of good and evil.

The Renaissance and the Age of Enlightenment saw a renewed interest in classical myths and legends, with writers such as Edmund Spenser, John Milton, and William Shakespeare incorporating mythical creatures into their works. For instance, Spenser's epic poem, The Faerie Queene, features a host of fantastical beings, including the dragon Errour, the witch Duessa, and the shape-shifting Archimago. These characters added a sense of wonder and magic to the narrative. They served as powerful human psyche symbols, representing the virtues and vices that define our moral character.

In the modern era, mythical creatures have continued to thrive in literature, with authors drawing on the rich tapestry of folklore and mythology to create new and imaginative worlds. For example, J.R.R. Tolkien's The Lord of the Rings is populated by a diverse array of mythical beings, from the noble Elves and the wise Ents to the fearsome Balrog and the monstrous Orcs. These creatures contribute to the epic scope and grandeur of Tolkien's Middle-earth and serve as potent metaphors for the forces of good and evil that shape our world.

Similarly, J.K. Rowling's Harry Potter series has introduced a new generation of readers to the wonders of mythical creatures, with magical beings such as the phoenix, the basilisk, and the hippogriff playing pivotal roles in the story. These creatures add a sense of enchantment and adventure to the narrative and are potent symbols of friendship, loyalty, and the triumph of good over evil.

In conclusion, the enduring presence of mythical creatures in literature is a testament to their timeless appeal and ability to resonate with readers across cultures and generations. From ancient epics to modern bestsellers, these fantastical beings have been powerful symbols and allegories, reflecting our deepest fears, desires, and aspirations. As we explore new frontiers in storytelling, it is clear that mythical creatures will remain an essential part of our literary landscape, inspiring and enchanting us for generations to come.

The Silver Screen: How Cinema Brought Mythical Creatures to Life

The magic of cinema has always been its ability to transport audiences to new worlds, and few things capture the imagination quite like mythical creatures. From the earliest days of film, these fantastical beings have played a significant role in storytelling, allowing filmmakers to explore themes of heroism, adventure, and the unknown. As technology has advanced, so too has the realism and complexity of these creatures, making them more lifelike and captivating than ever before.

In the early days of cinema, mythical creatures were often portrayed using stop-motion animation. This technique involved manipulating small models frame by frame to create the illusion of movement. This method was used to great effect in films such as "The Lost World" (1925) and "King Kong" (1933), which featured giant prehistoric creatures and a colossal ape, respectively. These films not only thrilled audiences with their groundbreaking special effects but also laid the foundation for future filmmakers to build upon.

As cinema evolved, so too did the portrayal of mythical creatures. The advent of color film allowed for more vibrant and imaginative depictions, as seen in classics like "The Wizard of Oz" (1939), which brought the mythical land of Oz and its inhabitants to life in vivid Technicolor. The 1950s and 1960s saw the rise of creature features, with films like "The Creature from the Black Lagoon" (1954) and "Jason and the Argonauts" (1963) showcasing a new generation of monsters and mythical beings.

The late 20th century saw a revolution in special effects, with the introduction of computer-generated imagery (CGI) allowing filmmakers to create more realistic and detailed creatures than ever before. This technology was used to stunning effect in films like "Jurassic Park" (1993), which brought dinosaurs back to life with unprecedented realism, and "The Lord of the Rings" trilogy (2001-2003), which featured a vast array of mythical beings from the noble elves to the fearsome Balrog.

In recent years, the popularity of mythical creatures in cinema has only continued to grow, with franchises like "Harry Potter" (2001-2011) and "The Chronicles of Narnia" (2005-2010) introducing a new generation of fans to the wonders of magical creatures and fantastical worlds. The success of these films has also led to a resurgence of interest in classic myths and legends, with films like "Clash of the Titans" (2010) and "Percy Jackson & the Olympians" (2010-2013) reimagining ancient tales for modern audiences.

The portrayal of mythical creatures in cinema has also significantly impacted other forms of media, with many films inspiring television shows, video games, and even theme park attractions. This cross-pollination of ideas has helped to keep mythical creatures at the forefront of popular culture, ensuring their continued relevance and appeal.

In conclusion, the silver screen has played a vital role in bringing mythical creatures to life, allowing audiences to experience the wonder and excitement of these fantastical beings in a way that was previously only possible through the pages of a book or the strokes of an artist's brush. As technology continues to advance, the portrayal of mythical creatures in cinema will likely become more immersive and captivating, ensuring their enduring place in the hearts and minds of audiences worldwide.

Television and the Rise of Fantasy Series: A New Platform for Mythical Beings

The advent of television has provided a new and powerful platform for mythical creatures to captivate audiences worldwide. As the medium evolved, so did the portrayal of these fantastical beings, with television series offering a unique opportunity to explore their stories in greater depth and detail than ever before. This section will delve into the rise of fantasy series and the role of mythical creatures within them, highlighting the impact of television on the way we perceive and engage with these timeless beings.

In the early days of television, mythical creatures were often relegated to the realm of children's programming, with shows like "The Adventures of Sir Lancelot" (1956) and "The Mighty Hercules" (1963) introducing young viewers to the legends of King Arthur and Greek mythology. However, as television matured, so too did its approach to the portrayal of mythical beings, with series like "The Twilight Zone" (1959-1964) and "Star Trek" (1966-1969) incorporating elements of mythology and folklore into their thought-provoking narratives.

The late 20th century saw the emergence of fantasy series that placed mythical creatures at the forefront of their storytelling. For example, "Buffy the Vampire Slayer" (1997-2003) and "Charmed" (1998-2006) both featured a diverse array of supernatural beings, from vampires and werewolves to demons and witches, while "Xena: Warrior Princess" (1995-2001) drew heavily on Greek mythology to create a rich and immersive world for its titular heroine.

The 21st century has witnessed an explosion of fantasy series that prominently feature mythical creatures, with shows like "Game of Thrones" (2011-2019), "American Gods" (2017-present), and "The Witcher" (2019-present) garnering critical acclaim and massive fan followings. These series have not only brought mythical beings to life with stunning visual effects but have also used them to explore complex themes and issues, such as power, morality, and identity.

Television has also played a significant role in the resurgence of interest in folklore and mythology, with series like "Grimm" (2011-2017) and "Supernatural" (2005-2020) drawing on centuries-old tales to create fresh and engaging narratives. These shows have introduced viewers to mythical creatures, from the familiar (such as werewolves and ghosts) to the lesser-known (such as the wendigo and the trickster).

The rise of fantasy series has provided a new platform for mythical beings and allowed for greater representation and diversity within the genre. Shows like "Merlin" (2008-2012) and "Penny Dreadful" (2014-2016) have featured characters from various cultural mythologies, while "Avatar: The Last Airbender" (2005-2008) and "The Dragon Prince" (2018-present) have incorporated elements of Eastern mythology and spirituality into their world-building.

In conclusion, television has played a crucial role in the ongoing fascination with mythical creatures, offering a unique and powerful platform for these beings to captivate and inspire audiences. The rise of fantasy series has brought these creatures to life in new and exciting ways and allowed for greater exploration of their stories, themes, and cultural significance. As the medium continues to evolve, it is clear that mythical creatures will remain an integral part of the television landscape, enchanting viewers for generations to come.

The World of Gaming: Interactive Encounters with Mythical Creatures

The gaming world has provided a unique and immersive platform for mythical creatures to thrive and captivate the imagination of players. Through interactive encounters, gamers can experience the wonder and excitement of these fantastical beings in a way that no other medium can offer. This section will explore how mythical creatures have been incorporated into video games, their impact on players, and the potential for future developments in this ever-evolving industry.

One of the earliest examples of mythical creatures in gaming can be traced back to the 1980s, with the release of the iconic role-playing game (RPG) series, "Dungeons & Dragons." This game allowed players to create their characters and embark on epic quests filled with mythical creatures such as dragons, unicorns, and griffins. The success of "Dungeons & Dragons" paved the way for other RPGs, such as "Final Fantasy" and "The Elder Scrolls," which also featured a plethora of mythical beings for players to encounter and interact with.

The rise of massively multiplayer online role-playing games (MMORPGs) like "World of Warcraft" and "Guild Wars" further expanded the presence of mythical creatures in gaming. These games not only allowed players to engage with mythical beings but also provided the opportunity to assume the role of one, such as a werewolf or a vampire. This level of immersion and interactivity has contributed to the enduring popularity of mythical creatures in the gaming world.

In addition to RPGs and MMORPGs, mythical creatures have also found their way into other gaming genres. For example, the "God of War" series, an action-adventure game, features the protagonist Kratos battling various creatures from Greek mythology, such as Medusa, the Minotaur, and the Hydra. Similarly, the "Assassin's Creed" franchise has incorporated mythical creatures from Egyptian, Greek, and Norse mythology into its historical settings, allowing players to experience these legends in a unique and engaging way.

The impact of mythical creatures in gaming goes beyond mere entertainment. These interactive encounters can foster a deeper appreciation and understanding of the myths and legends from which they originate. By engaging with these creatures in a virtual environment, players can develop a more profound connection to the stories and cultures that have shaped human history.

The future of mythical creatures in gaming is full of potential. With the advent of virtual reality (VR) and augmented reality (AR) technologies, players can expect even more immersive and realistic experiences with mythical beings. Imagine exploring a VR world where you can come face-to-face with a fire-breathing dragon or an AR game that allows you to capture and train your mythical creatures in the real world. The possibilities are endless, and the continued fascination with mythical creatures ensures they will remain a prominent feature in the gaming landscape for years.

In conclusion, gaming has provided a unique and interactive platform for mythical creatures to captivate and engage players. From RPGs to action-adventure games, these fantastical beings have become an integral part of the gaming experience, fostering a deeper appreciation for the myths and legends that have shaped human history. As technology advances, the future of mythical creatures in gaming promises to be even more immersive and exciting, ensuring their enduring presence in interactive entertainment.

Art and Design: The Aesthetic Influence of Mythical Beings

Mythical creatures have long captivated the human imagination, inspiring countless artists and designers throughout history. From the intricate carvings of ancient temples to the fantastical illustrations in modern graphic novels, the aesthetic influence of mythical beings is undeniable. In this section, we will explore how these enigmatic creatures have shaped the world of art and design, leaving an indelible mark on our visual culture.

The earliest examples of mythical creatures in art can be traced back to the cave paintings of prehistoric times. These primitive depictions of fantastical beasts and hybrid creatures were a testament to the power of human imagination and our innate desire to explore the unknown. As civilizations developed, so too did the artistic representation of mythical beings. The ancient Egyptians, Greeks, and Romans incorporated mythical creatures into their art and architecture, using them as symbols of power, wisdom, and protection.

In the Middle Ages, mythical creatures found their way into the illuminated manuscripts and tapestries of the time. These intricate works of art often featured dragons, unicorns, and other fantastical beings, serving as decorative elements and allegorical symbols. The Renaissance saw a resurgence of interest in mythology, with artists like Leonardo da Vinci and Michelangelo incorporating mythical creatures into their masterpieces.

The aesthetic influence of mythical beings continued to evolve with the advent of new artistic movements and styles. Romanticism, for example, embraced the fantastical and mysterious, with artists like William Blake and Gustave Doré creating hauntingly beautiful depictions of mythical creatures. The Art Nouveau movement, with its emphasis on organic forms and flowing lines, also found inspiration in the world of mythology, as seen in the works of Alphonse Mucha and René Lalique.

In design, mythical creatures have been a popular motif for centuries. From the ornate dragon motifs in Chinese ceramics to the whimsical fairy illustrations of Victorian-era children's books, these fantastical beings have been used to add a touch of magic and wonder to everyday objects. In more recent times, the influence of mythical creatures can be seen in the fashion world, with designers like Alexander McQueen and Iris van Herpen drawing inspiration from the shapes, textures, and stories of these enigmatic beings.

The digital age has opened up new possibilities for the artistic representation of mythical creatures. With the advent of computer-generated imagery (CGI) and virtual reality, artists and designers can now create incredibly lifelike and immersive depictions of mythical beings, blurring the lines between fantasy and reality. This has led to a resurgence of interest in mythical creatures, as seen in the popularity of movies, video games, and graphic novels featuring these fantastical beings.

In conclusion, the aesthetic influence of mythical beings is deeply ingrained in our visual culture, transcending time and artistic styles. From the earliest cave paintings to the cutting-edge digital art of today, these enigmatic creatures continue to captivate our imagination and inspire us to push the boundaries of creativity. As we look to the future, it is clear that the timeless allure of mythical creatures will continue to shape the world of art and design, enchanting generations to come.

Fashion and Mythology: The Inspiration Behind Trendsetting Styles

The fashion world has always been a melting pot of creativity, drawing inspiration from various sources, including art, history, and culture. One such source that has significantly influenced the fashion industry is mythology. The enchanting tales and captivating imagery of mythical creatures have left an indelible mark on the minds of designers, leading to the creation of trendsetting styles that continue to captivate audiences worldwide.

Mythical creatures have long been a source of fascination for their unique characteristics, otherworldly beauty, and the symbolism they represent. Fashion designers have tapped into this allure, using these fantastical beings as muses for their collections. From the ethereal elegance of nymphs and fairies to the fierce power of dragons and griffins, the influence of mythology on fashion is undeniable.

One of the most iconic examples of mythology-inspired fashion is the late Alexander McQueen's 2010 collection, "Plato's Atlantis." Drawing inspiration from the myth of the lost city of Atlantis, McQueen's designs featured intricate prints of sea creatures, iridescent fabrics, and avant-garde silhouettes that evoked the mysterious underwater world. The collection showcased the designer's ability to transform ancient myths into modern, cutting-edge fashion.

Another notable instance of mythology's impact on fashion is the regular use of Medusa's image in the Versace logo. The Italian luxury brand, founded by Gianni Versace, chose the mythical Gorgon as its emblem, symbolizing power, strength, and beauty. As a result, Medusa's snake-entwined visage has become synonymous with the brand, appearing on clothing, accessories, and even the runway itself.

The influence of mythical creatures extends beyond high fashion into streetwear and casual clothing. Dragons, unicorns, and other fantastical beings have found their way onto graphic tees, hoodies, and sneakers, making them accessible to a broader audience. These designs often incorporate elements of pop culture, blending the ancient with the contemporary to create a unique and appealing aesthetic.

Fashion and mythology also intersect in the form of wearable art, such as jewelry and accessories. Designers have crafted stunning pieces inspired by mythical creatures, from delicate fairy wing earrings to bold, statement-making dragon necklaces. These wearable works of art allow individuals to express their affinity for mythology and its captivating creatures subtly yet stylishly.

The relationship between fashion and mythology is not merely one of aesthetic inspiration; it also serves as a means of storytelling and self-expression. By incorporating mythical creatures into their designs, fashion designers invite their audiences to explore the rich tapestry of myths and legends that have shaped human history. In doing so, they connect the wearer and the ancient world, allowing them to embody these timeless beings' power, beauty, and mystique.

In conclusion, the influence of mythical creatures on fashion is a testament to their enduring appeal and the power of storytelling. As designers continue to draw inspiration from these fantastical beings, we can expect to see even more innovative and captivating styles that pay homage to the rich world of mythology. The fusion of fashion and mythology not only results in trendsetting styles but also serves as a reminder of the timeless significance of these enchanting creatures in our modern culture and media.

The Role of Mythical Creatures in Advertising and Branding

Mythical creatures have long captured the imagination of people across the globe, transcending cultural and geographical boundaries. Their enigmatic nature and otherworldly allure make them powerful advertising and branding tools. This section will explore how mythical creatures have been utilized in various marketing campaigns and the reasons behind their enduring appeal in the advertising industry.

One of the primary reasons mythical creatures are employed in advertising is their ability to evoke strong emotions and create a sense of wonder. By incorporating these fantastical beings into their campaigns, brands can instantly capture the attention of their target audience and create a memorable impression. For instance, using a majestic unicorn in a commercial can evoke feelings of magic, purity, and enchantment, while a fierce dragon can symbolize power, strength, and mystery.

Another advantage of using mythical creatures in advertising is their versatility. These beings can be adapted to suit the specific needs of a brand or product, allowing marketers to create a unique and captivating narrative. For example, a company selling energy drinks might use a mythical creature like the phoenix to represent their product's rejuvenating and invigorating effects. Similarly, a luxury car brand could use a mythical creature like the griffin, a symbol of nobility and power, to convey their vehicles' high status and prestige.

Mythical creatures also serve as a powerful visual element in advertising, allowing brands to create eye-catching and distinctive designs. Using these beings in logos, packaging, and promotional materials can help a brand stand out from its competitors and create a solid visual identity. For instance, the Starbucks logo features a mermaid-like creature called a siren, which has become an iconic symbol of the brand and is instantly recognizable to consumers worldwide.

In addition to their visual appeal, mythical creatures can also be used to convey a brand's values and ethos. By aligning themselves with a particular mythical being, companies can communicate their brand's personality and create a deeper emotional connection with their audience. For example, a brand that values sustainability and environmental conservation might use a mythical creature like the earth-loving nymph to represent its commitment to protecting the planet.

Moreover, the use of mythical creatures in advertising can also tap into a sense of nostalgia and cultural heritage. Many of these beings have their roots in ancient folklore and mythology, and their inclusion in modern marketing campaigns can evoke a sense of familiarity and tradition. This can be particularly effective for brands that wish to emphasize their long-standing history or cultural significance.

In conclusion, the role of mythical creatures in advertising and branding is multifaceted and enduring. These fantastical beings offer a unique combination of visual appeal, emotional resonance, and cultural significance, making them a powerful tool for capturing the attention and imagination of consumers. As the advertising world continues to evolve, mythical creatures will likely remain a popular and effective means of communication for brands seeking to create a lasting impact on their audience.

Mythical Creatures as Cultural Symbols: National Identity and Heritage

Mythical creatures have long been a part of human history, with their stories and legends passed down through generations. These fantastical beings have not only captured our imaginations but have also become deeply ingrained in our cultural identities. In this section, we will explore the role of mythical creatures as symbols of national identity and heritage and how they continue to shape our understanding of the world around us.

Across the globe, mythical creatures have been adopted as emblems of national pride and identity. For instance, the dragon is a powerful symbol in Chinese culture, representing strength, wisdom, and good fortune. It is often depicted in traditional art, architecture, and even in the design of the Chinese New Year celebrations. Similarly, the unicorn, a symbol of purity and grace, is an integral part of Scottish folklore and has been the national animal of Scotland since the 12th century. The image of the unicorn can be found on the Scottish royal coat of arms and on various official documents and buildings.

In addition to their symbolic significance, mythical creatures also link to our shared cultural heritage. They connect us to our ancestors and their stories, providing a sense of continuity and belonging. For example, the Native American Thunderbird is a legendary creature deeply rooted in North America's indigenous cultures. The Thunderbird is believed to be a powerful supernatural being that controls the elements, particularly thunder, and lightning. Its presence in various tribal myths and legends serves as a reminder of the rich cultural history of the Native American people.

Mythical creatures also play a crucial role in preserving and promoting cultural diversity. Each culture has its unique set of mythical beings, which serve as a testament to the richness and variety of human imagination and creativity. By celebrating and sharing these stories, we honor our heritage and foster a greater understanding and appreciation of other cultures.

In the modern era, the significance of mythical creatures as cultural symbols has not diminished. On the contrary, they have become even more prominent as countries and communities seek to assert their unique identities in an increasingly globalized world. As a result, festivals, parades, and other cultural events often feature these mythical beings, showcasing their importance in the people's collective consciousness.

Moreover, the resurgence of interest in folklore and mythology has led to a renewed appreciation for the role of mythical creatures in shaping our cultural narratives. Books, movies, and television series that draw inspiration from these ancient tales have introduced a new generation to the wonders of these legendary beings, ensuring that their stories continue to be passed down and cherished.

In conclusion, mythical creatures are unique and enduring in our cultural landscape. As national identity and heritage symbols, they connect to our past and are a source of pride in our shared history. By embracing and celebrating these fantastical beings, we preserve our cultural heritage and contribute to a richer, more diverse understanding of the world around us.

The Psychological Impact of Mythical Creatures on Society

Mythical creatures have long captured the imagination of people across cultures and generations. These fantastical beings, often possessing extraordinary powers and abilities, have become deeply ingrained in our collective consciousness. The psychological impact of mythical creatures on society is multifaceted, as they symbolize our deepest fears, desires, and aspirations. In this section, we will explore how mythical creatures have shaped our understanding of the world and ourselves.

One of the mythical creatures' most significant psychological effects is their ability to embody and personify human emotions and experiences. By attributing human characteristics to these otherworldly beings, we can better comprehend and process complex emotions such as love, jealousy, anger, and grief. For example, the Greek myth of Medusa, a woman cursed with snakes for hair and a gaze that turns people to stone, can be interpreted as a metaphor for the destructive power of envy and bitterness. Similarly, the story of the phoenix, a mythical bird that is cyclically reborn from its ashes, symbolizes the resilience and transformative power of the human spirit.

Mythical creatures also serve as a means of exploring societal norms and values. They often embody moral lessons and cautionary tales, warning against the dangers of hubris, greed, and other vices. For instance, the tale of Icarus, who flew too close to the sun with his wax wings and fell to his death, teaches the importance of moderation and humility. By presenting these lessons through the lens of mythical creatures, we can engage with these moral teachings more imaginatively and memorably.

Furthermore, mythical creatures provide a sense of wonder and escapism, allowing us to suspend our disbelief and immerse ourselves in fantastical worlds temporarily. This can be particularly beneficial in times of stress or hardship, as engaging with these stories can offer a form of emotional catharsis and a reprieve from the challenges of everyday life. The enduring popularity of fantasy literature, films, and television series is a testament to the psychological appeal of mythical creatures and the worlds they inhabit.

In addition to their role as symbols and vehicles for storytelling, mythical creatures can also serve as powerful archetypes that resonate with our subconscious minds. The psychologist Carl Jung believed that mythical creatures and other archetypal figures are part of the collective unconscious, a shared reservoir of symbols and images that are universally recognized and understood. By tapping into these archetypes, stories featuring mythical creatures can evoke deep emotional responses and foster a sense of connection and shared experience among audiences.

In conclusion, mythical creatures' psychological impact on society is profound and multifaceted. These fantastical beings allow us to explore and process complex emotions, impart moral lessons, provide a sense of wonder and escapism, and tap into powerful archetypal symbols that resonate with our subconscious minds. As our world continues to evolve and change, mythical creatures will likely play a significant role in shaping our understanding of ourselves and the world around us.

The Future of Mythical Creatures in Media: New Technologies and Storytelling Techniques

As we venture further into the 21st century, the role of mythical creatures in modern culture and media continues to evolve and expand. With the rapid advancement of technology and the emergence of new storytelling techniques, these fantastical beings are finding new ways to captivate and enchant audiences worldwide. In this section, we will explore the future of mythical creatures in media, focusing on the innovative technologies and narrative methods that will shape their portrayal and influence in the years to come.

One of the most significant developments in recent years is the rise of virtual reality (VR) and augmented reality (AR) technologies. These immersive platforms offer unprecedented opportunities for creators to bring mythical creatures to life in vivid and interactive ways. Imagine donning a VR headset and stepping into a fantastical world where you can interact with dragons, unicorns, or other mythical beings in a fully realized environment. Similarly, AR technology allows users to overlay digital images of mythical creatures onto their real-world surroundings, creating a seamless blend of reality and fantasy. As a result, we expect to see more immersive and engaging experiences featuring our favorite mythical creatures as these technologies advance.

Another promising development is the growing popularity of interactive storytelling, particularly in video games. As gaming technology becomes more sophisticated, so does the potential for complex and engaging narratives that innovatively incorporate mythical creatures. Players can now assume the roles of these fantastical beings, shaping their stories and influencing their worlds in previously unimaginable ways. This level of interactivity deepens our connection to these creatures and allows for a more profound exploration of their mythologies and cultural significance.

Artificial intelligence (AI) and machine learning are also poised to revolutionize how we engage with mythical creatures in media. These technologies can create dynamic, responsive narratives that adapt to individual users' preferences and choices. This could lead to highly personalized experiences, where mythical creatures and their stories are tailored to each person's unique interests and sensibilities. Additionally, AI-generated content could create entirely new mythical creatures born from the collective imagination of countless users and shaped by ever-evolving algorithms.

Finally, the future of mythical creatures in media will be heavily influenced by the continued globalization of culture and the increasing interconnectedness of our world. As creators and audiences become more diverse and inclusive, we can expect to see a broader range of mythical creatures from various cultural traditions represented in media. This will enrich our understanding of these fantastical beings and foster greater appreciation and respect for the diverse cultures that have given rise to them.

In conclusion, the future of mythical creatures in modern culture and media is bright and full of potential. As technology advances and new storytelling techniques emerge, these timeless beings will find innovative ways to captivate and inspire us. Whether through immersive VR experiences, interactive gaming narratives, AI-generated content, or the celebration of diverse cultural traditions, mythical creatures will undoubtedly continue to play a significant role in shaping our collective imagination and enriching our lives.

The Timeless Significance of Mythical Creatures in Modern Culture and Media

In conclusion, the timeless significance of mythical creatures in modern culture and media is undeniable. These fantastical beings have captivated the human imagination for centuries, transcending geographical boundaries and evolving through various forms of storytelling. From ancient epics to contemporary bestsellers, mythical creatures have played a pivotal role in shaping the narratives that define our collective consciousness.

The advent of cinema, television, and gaming has only served to amplify the presence of mythical creatures in our lives, allowing us to interact with them in new and exciting ways. These platforms have brought these beings to life and provided a space for them to evolve and adapt to the changing tastes and preferences of modern audiences. The aesthetic influence of mythical creatures can also be seen in various aspects of art and design and in the fashion industry, where they continue to inspire trendsetting styles.

Moreover, mythical creatures have become powerful symbols of national identity and heritage, serving as a testament to the rich cultural history of different societies. They have also found their way into the world of advertising and branding, where they are used to evoke a sense of wonder and curiosity in consumers.

The psychological impact of mythical creatures on society is also worth noting, as they often embody our deepest fears, desires, and aspirations. They serve as a mirror to our humanity, reflecting our strengths and weaknesses and reminding us of the power of storytelling to shape our understanding of the world around us.

As we look to the future, it is clear that mythical creatures will continue to play a significant role in media and culture. Emerging technologies and innovative storytelling techniques will undoubtedly provide new opportunities for these beings to enchant and inspire future generations. Virtual reality, augmented reality, and artificial intelligence are just a few examples of technological advancements that have the potential to revolutionize the way we engage with mythical creatures.

In essence, the enduring appeal of mythical creatures lies in their ability to transport us to a world of wonder and possibility, where the boundaries between reality and fantasy are blurred. They serve as a reminder of the power of imagination and the importance of preserving the rich tapestry of myths and legends that have shaped human history. As long as there are stories to be told, mythical creatures will continue to hold a special place in our hearts and minds, captivating us with their timeless allure and shaping the cultural landscape for generations to come.

THE ENDURING FASCINATION WITH MYTHICAL CREATURES

As we reach the end of our journey through the enchanting world of mythical creatures, it is essential to pause and reflect on the purpose of this epilogue. Throughout the book, we have explored the rich tapestry of legends, folklore, and mythology that has given birth to many fantastical beings. From the fearsome dragons of the East to the enigmatic mermaids of the deep, these creatures have captured the imagination of countless generations, transcending the boundaries of time and culture.

This concluding chapter aims to weave together the various threads of our exploration, highlighting the major themes and findings that have emerged from our study of these mythical beings. We will delve into the implications and significance of these creatures in shaping human society and culture and address the limitations and critiques that inevitably arise in any scholarly endeavor. Finally, we will offer some thoughts and recommendations for future research and engagement with the captivating realm of mythical creatures.

In doing so, we hope to provide a fitting conclusion to our journey, which celebrates the enduring fascination with these magical beings and encourages readers to continue exploring the vast and wondrous world of mythology. So, let us embark on this final leg of our adventure as we seek to unravel the threads of mythical narratives and uncover the profound impact that these creatures have had on the human experience.

Unraveling the Threads of Mythical Narratives

Throughout this book, we have embarked on a fascinating journey, exploring the rich tapestry of mythical creatures that have captivated the human imagination for centuries. As we conclude our exploration, we must take a step back and reflect on the major themes and findings that have emerged from our study of these enigmatic beings. By doing so, we can better understand the enduring fascination with mythical creatures and their significance in our collective consciousness.

One of the most striking themes that has emerged from our examination of mythical creatures is the universality of their presence across cultures and time periods. From the ancient Greek tales of centaurs and sirens to the Native American legends of thunderbirds and skinwalkers, it is evident that the human imagination has consistently given birth to fantastical beings that defy the boundaries of the natural world. This widespread phenomenon suggests that something deeply ingrained in the human psyche compels us to create and share stories of mythical creatures.

Another key finding from our study is the remarkable diversity and complexity of mythical creatures. Far from mere figments of the imagination, these beings often embody various human emotions, desires, and fears. For example, the ferocious dragons of European folklore can be seen as symbols of chaos and destruction, while the benevolent unicorns represent purity and innocence. This multifaceted nature of mythical creatures allows them to serve as powerful vehicles for exploring the complexities of the human experience.

Furthermore, our exploration of mythical creatures has revealed their important role in shaping cultural identity and preserving traditional beliefs. Many mythical creatures are deeply rooted in the folklore and mythology of specific cultures, serving as embodiments of their values, history, and worldview. For instance, the legendary phoenix of ancient Egypt and Greece symbolizes the cyclical nature of life and the power of rebirth, reflecting the ancient civilizations' beliefs in the afterlife and the eternal nature of the soul.

In addition to their cultural significance, mythical creatures also serve as potent sources of inspiration and creativity in various forms of art and literature. From the epic poems of Homer to the fantastical realms of J.R.R. Tolkien and J.K. Rowling, mythical creatures have long captivated the minds of writers, artists, and audiences alike. By transcending the limitations of reality, these beings invite us to explore the boundless possibilities of the imagination and challenge our perceptions of the world around us.

In conclusion, our journey through the world of mythical creatures has unveiled a rich and diverse landscape of fantastical beings that continue to captivate the human imagination. By examining our study's major themes and findings, we can gain a deeper appreciation for the enduring fascination with mythical creatures and their significance in our collective consciousness. As we continue to explore the realm of myth and legend, we can look forward to uncovering even more insights into the mysterious allure of these enigmatic beings.

The Impact of Mythical Creatures on Society and Culture

Throughout history, mythical creatures have captivated the human imagination, leaving an indelible mark on our collective consciousness. These fantastical beings have entertained and inspired us and played a significant role in shaping our society and culture. In this section, we will delve into the implications and significance of mythical creatures, exploring how they have influenced our world.

First and foremost, mythical creatures have served as powerful symbols and metaphors, embodying different cultures' values, fears, and aspirations. For instance, the dragon has been a potent symbol of power and wisdom in Chinese mythology, while the phoenix represents rebirth and renewal in Greek and Egyptian myths. By personifying abstract concepts and emotions, mythical creatures have allowed us to understand better and navigate the complexities of the human experience.

Moreover, mythical creatures have played a crucial role in fostering a sense of cultural identity and continuity. The stories and legends surrounding these beings have been passed down through generations as a link between the past and the present. By preserving and retelling these tales, we honor our ancestors and their beliefs and ensure that the rich tapestry of our cultural heritage remains intact for future generations to appreciate.

In addition to their symbolic and cultural significance, mythical creatures have profoundly impacted the arts and literature. From the epic poems of ancient Greece to the fantasy novels of today, these beings have been a constant source of inspiration for writers, poets, and artists. They have given rise to countless works of art, music, and theater, enriching our lives and expanding our understanding of the world.

Furthermore, the study of mythical creatures has contributed to the development of various academic disciplines, including anthropology, folklore, and psychology. By examining these beings' origins, evolution, and cultural significance, scholars have gained valuable insights into the human psyche and how we make sense of the world. This interdisciplinary approach has not only deepened our knowledge of mythical creatures but has also shed light on the broader patterns and processes that underlie human culture and cognition.

Lastly, it is worth noting that mythical creatures continue to hold a special place in our hearts and minds, even in today's increasingly rational and scientific world. They serve as a reminder of the power of imagination and the enduring appeal of the unknown, inviting us to explore the boundaries of our reality and to question the limits of our understanding. In this sense, mythical creatures enrich our cultural landscape and challenge us to think more critically and creatively about the world we inhabit.

In conclusion, the impact of mythical creatures on society and culture is vast and multifaceted, spanning the realms of symbolism, cultural identity, art, academia, and beyond. By examining how these beings have shaped our world, we can better appreciate their enduring fascination and their important role in our lives.

Addressing the Inevitable Shortcomings and Counterarguments

As we delve into the realm of mythical creatures, it is essential to acknowledge the limitations and critiques that inevitably arise in studying such a diverse and complex subject matter. By addressing these concerns, we can better understand the nuances of our fascination with mythical beings and strive for a more comprehensive and balanced perspective.

One of the primary limitations in studying mythical creatures is the vast array of cultural and historical contexts from which they emerge. With countless myths and legends spanning the globe, it is impossible to provide an exhaustive analysis of every mythical creature that has ever been conceived. As such, our exploration has focused on a selection of 100 mythical creatures, which, while extensive, is not comprehensive. This limitation highlights the need for further research and exploration into lesser-known myths and legends that may reveal more fascinating creatures and the stories surrounding them.

Another critique often leveled at the study of mythical creatures is the subjective nature of interpreting these beings and their significance. As myths and legends are often passed down through oral tradition, they are subject to change and reinterpretation over time. This fluidity can make it challenging to pinpoint the original intent or meaning behind a particular creature, leading to multiple interpretations and potential misunderstandings. To address this concern, we have endeavored to provide a balanced analysis of each creature, drawing on various sources and perspectives to offer a well-rounded understanding of their role and significance within their respective cultural contexts.

Additionally, some critics argue that studying mythical creatures is an exercise in frivolity, as these beings are ultimately fictional and hold no tangible bearing on the real world. While it is true that mythical creatures do not exist in a literal sense, their impact on society and culture cannot be dismissed. As we have explored throughout this book, mythical creatures serve as powerful symbols and allegories, reflecting the values, fears, and aspirations of the cultures that create them. By examining these creatures and the stories surrounding them, we gain valuable insights into the human experience and how we make sense of the world around us.

Lastly, it is essential to recognize that our cultural biases and preconceptions shape our understanding of mythical creatures. Therefore, as researchers and enthusiasts, we must approach these beings with an open mind and a willingness to challenge our assumptions. By doing so, we can foster a more inclusive and nuanced understanding of the rich tapestry of myths and legends that have captivated the human imagination for millennia.

In conclusion, while the study of mythical creatures is not without its limitations and critiques, these challenges serve as opportunities for growth and deeper understanding. By acknowledging and addressing these concerns, we can continue to explore the fascinating world of mythical beings and the enduring allure they hold for us all.

Charting a Path Forward in the Study of Mythical Beings

As we reach the end of our journey through the world of mythical creatures, it is essential to reflect on the significance of these beings in our collective imagination and consider the future of their study. Throughout this book, we have explored the rich tapestry of myths and legends that have captivated the human spirit for centuries. From the majestic dragons of the East to the enigmatic mermaids of the Deep, these creatures have served as symbols of our fears, desires, and aspirations.

In this final section, we offer recommendations for those who wish to delve deeper into the study of mythical beings and contribute to the ongoing conversation about their role in our lives.

First and foremost, it is crucial to approach the study of mythical creatures with an open mind and a willingness to embrace the diverse perspectives that have shaped their narratives. This requires a commitment to interdisciplinary research, as the stories of these beings are woven into the fabric of history, literature, art, and religion. By drawing on the insights of scholars from various fields, we can better understand the cultural and psychological forces that have given rise to these enduring legends.

Second, we encourage researchers to explore the connections between mythical creatures and contemporary issues. As we have seen throughout this book, the stories of these beings often reflect the concerns and values of the societies in which they were created. By examining how mythical creatures have been adapted and reimagined in modern contexts, we can gain valuable insights into how our culture grapples with questions of identity, power, and the unknown.

Third, we recommend that scholars continue to engage with the rich body of primary sources that document the stories of mythical creatures. From ancient texts and oral traditions to visual representations in art and media, these sources offer information about how these beings have been imagined and interpreted over time. By critically analyzing these materials, we can uncover the layers of meaning that have shaped our understanding of mythical creatures and their significance in our lives.

Finally, we urge researchers to consider the ethical implications of their work in the study of mythical beings. As we have discussed in this book, the stories of these creatures are often deeply intertwined with issues of power, identity, and cultural appropriation. By approaching our research with sensitivity and respect for the diverse communities that have contributed to the rich tapestry of myths and legends, we can ensure that our scholarship contributes to a more inclusive and equitable understanding of the world's cultural heritage.

In conclusion, the enduring fascination with mythical creatures offers a unique opportunity to explore the depths of human imagination and the complex interplay of cultural, psychological, and historical forces that have shaped our understanding of the world. By charting a path forward in studying these beings, we can continue to unravel the mysteries of our collective past and, perhaps, catch a glimpse of the future that awaits us.

ABOUT THE AUTHOR

Luke Marsh, a passionate philosopher and critical thinker, has now ventured into the realm of trivia and fascinating facts with his latest series, "The Ultimate 100 Series". Known for his deep love for exploring the complexities of the world, Luke has spent years delving into the depths of philosophical thought, which has now translated into a series that explores the most intriguing, bizarre, and awe-inspiring aspects of our world. Each book in this exhilarating series is a testament to Luke's curiosity and knack for uncovering the extraordinary in the ordinary. When he's not writing or thinking deeply, Luke can be found outdoors, spending time with loved ones, or lost in a good book. With "The Ultimate 100 Series", Luke invites you to join him on a rollercoaster ride of discovery, perfect for trivia buffs, curious minds, and adventure seekers alike.

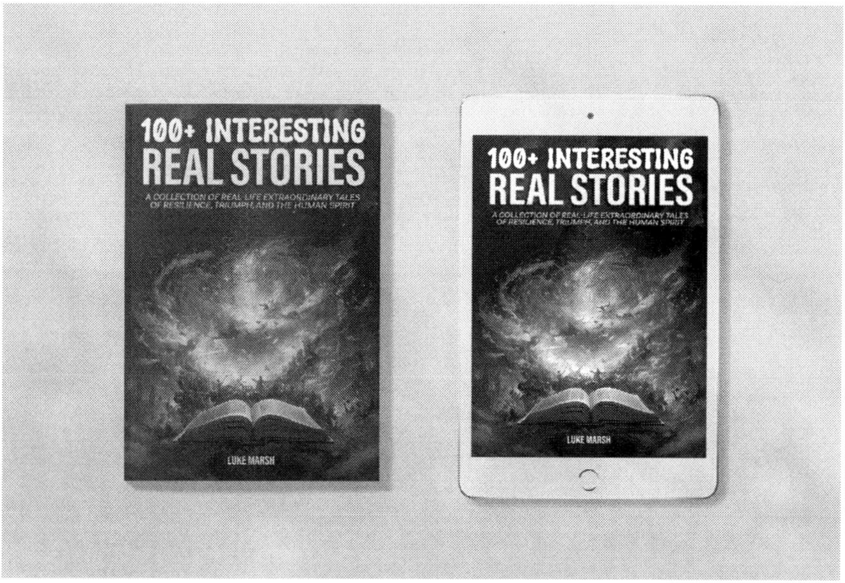

Made in the USA
Columbia, SC
09 February 2025

d949fb39-110b-480e-86ea-d66328820f5fR01